Real Life

Gangsters

Pablo Escobar

and Al Capone

2 Books in 1

Roger Harrington

PABLO ESCOBAR
Narcos King

The World's Most
Infamous Gangster

Roger Harrington

Table of Contents

A Corpse On A Rooftop

The city of Medellin is the second-largest in the South American nation of Columbia. It is nestled in the Aburra Valley in the Andes ranges.

On December 2 1992 citizens of the district of Los Olivos heard gunshots from the rooftops. They saw two men running across the orange – tiled roofs, pursued by a group of armed and uniformed men.

A short gunfight ensued. Soon eight armed men, officers of the National Columbian Police, posed for photographs, brandishing weapons and smiling over the bloody corpse of a 44-year-old man.

That man was Pablo Emilia Escobar Gaviria, known in the annals of infamy simply as Pablo Escobar.

He had been the most powerful drug lord in Colombia and one of the most notorious in the world.

He was so pernicious that for a time he was number one on the hit list of the United States. He controlled the cocaine trade in the United States.

He used wealth and terror to dominate Columbian politics and destroy his enemies.

He openly flaunted his fantastic wealth, believing that he was untouchable.

But there he was, a bare-footed, bloody corpse, his executioners shouting 'Viva Columbia! Viva Columbia!'

So who was this man?

Pablo Escobar was born on November 1 1949 in the Columbian city of Rionegro.

His father, Abel de Jesus Dari Escobar was a peasant father of moderate means.

His mother was Hermilda Gaviria, a school teacher.

Pablo was the third of seven children.

His parents were poor and suffered hardship. Pablo had to work far to school and he had only one pair of shoes. When these wore out he walked barefoot.

He was humiliated by his teacher and sent back home. Hermilda had no money to buy shoes and so stole some.

Smitten by remorse she confessed to a priest and returned the shoes. She was allowed to buy a pair on credit.

Pablo comforted his mother, saying 'Don't worry, mom, wait until I grow up, I will give you everything.'

Pablo's father was away for long periods in the field. His mother not only had to look after seven children but hold down her job as a teacher.

The Gaviria children had to learn independence and resilience in their hard world.

There were light moments, however, such as when their mother would regale them with stories of their paternal grandfather Roberto, who was a whiskey smuggler.

In these stories the wily Roberto would always outwit the authorities with new and adventurous schemes.

During Pablo's childhood Columbia was in the throes of a civil war. From 1948 to 1958 the Columbian Conservative Party and the Columbian Liberal Party fought for control of the country.

About 25,000 armed combatants perished in the conflict, but the brunt of the savagery was born by the civilian population. Millions were forced to flee their homes and abandon their property. Up to 300,000 were killed.

This terrible conflict was called simply *La Violencia*. Bloodletting and torture became so familiar to the people that names for them entered the Columbian lexicon.

Pica para tamal was the slow cutting away of flesh from someone until they died.

Bochachiquiar involved inflicting tiny punctures, causing the victim to slowly bleed to death.

Then there was the *Corbata Columbiana* or Columbian neck-tie, where the victim's tongue would be pulled through a horizontal slash in the victim's neck.

Crucifixions were commonplace. People were thrown from planes in mid-flight. Schoolgirls as young as eight were raped. Infants were torn from their mothers' wombs and replaced by roosters.

Children were bayonetted. Ears were cut off. The barbarities seemed endless.

A child growing up in these times might very well be accustomed to violence as a way of life.

La Violencia was precipitated by the assassination of Jorge Gatan, the leader of the Liberal Party and a presidential candidate in 1948.

It was widely believed that the CIA was responsible for the killing. The United States did indeed have an interest in keeping the anti-Communist Conservative Party in power.

The death of a populist leader who had pledged to help the poor, ostensibly at the hands of the US must have influenced the boy Escobar's anti-US views later on.

From an early age Pablo had drive and ambition. He wanted to rise above his condition. He wanted to become President of Columbia by the age of 30. He also wanted to become a millionaire by the age of 22.

It seems however that from an early age he chose a criminal path toward success.

As a child he was engaged in street crime.

As a teenager he stole gravestones and sanded them down for resale. He also sold counterfeit high school diplomas and stole cars.

There was a side to Escobar that was socially conscious. At the tender age of 13 he was elected President of his school's Council for Student Wellness. This group advocated for the poor.

He rebelled against authority. He began to skip school. When his mother discovered that he had not attended school in 2 years she sent him back.

Escobar protested. He preferred the education the Medellin gangs could give him. 'Mother, I keep on telling you, I want to be big, I want to be big,' he said. 'And I will be… I'm poor but I will never die poor, I promise.'

Inevitably he was expelled and he settled into lie as a street criminal.

As a youth he vowed to rise above his own poverty and labor against poverty. Later in life he would be known to many of the poor in Columbia as their nation's Robin Hood.

Escobar did go to the Universidad Autónoma Latinoamericana in Medellin. This seemed strange given his disillusionment with traditional education. Perhaps he believed a future President of Columbia would need a degree. Whatever the motivation, he left without obtaining it.

By the age of 20 Escobar was already a legend in Medellin. His cool, dead-pan style of robbing banks without even threatening the bank teller with the rifle he carried attracted men to him.

Soon he had his own gang. One of these first gang members said 'He was like a God, a man with a very powerful aura. When I met him for the first time it was the most important day of my life.'

From now on, he would never again dirty his own hands. Instead he had only to command something and it would be done.

Escobar's Columbia

Columbia has a long history of violence and political instability.

In 1819, after a period of war, the Spanish Viceroyalty of New Granada became an independent republic, Granada.

Soon the country was divided between Conservatives and Liberals. Both parties struggled for power and both parties produced presidents for Columbia. Violent conflict between them was sporadic.

A terrible civil war erupted between the two in 1899. The Thousand Days War, which lasted 1,130 days, ended the lives of 120,000 Columbians. This was from a population of little more than 4,200 000.

Child soldiers featured in this conflict, as in the most of the nineteenth-century conflicts in Columbia.

We have already seen the origins of *La Violencia*. It ended in 1958 when Conservatives and Liberals agreed to share government. This 'National Front' government would have alternating Liberal and Conservative Presidents, each running for four-year terms for 16 years.

This arrangement did not satisfy all however.

Disaffected Liberal and Communist peasant communities formed armed bands which fought National Front forces.

These units coalesced into the Revolutionary Armed Forces of Columbia, or FARC.

There were also Far Right paramilitary groups.

Both sides financed themselves by kidnapping and drug trafficking.

The United States government was keenly interested in Columbian politics. Columbia is in the north-west of South America and borders the Panama Isthmus, the narrow stretch of land that joins South America to North America.

In fact the small nation of Panama had been part of Columbia until it declared independence, with US support, in 1903. Panama granted permission to the United States to build the Panama Canal and also granted the US sovereign rights over the canal.

The Panama Canal is an important conduit of trade for the United States and its integrity is vital to its interests.

The regime in Columbia is therefore of great interest to the United States.

During the Cold War it sought to protect the canal from Communist influence and protect US business interests in Columbia, and so supported Conservative forces in Columbia.

This then was the Columbia in which hundreds of thousands of poor youths of Escobar's generation grew up in – crippled by poverty, torn by factions and rendered lawless by armed thugs, drug lords and terrorists.

It was a major battleground of the Cold War and became the plaything of international capitalism and communism.

Many of these youths, Escobar included, experienced a regime bathed in blood and mired in corruption since before they were born. It could offer them no hope.

So they turned to crime.

Rise To Power

Drug trafficking was rife in Escobar's Colombia. As we have mentioned, it was a major source of financing for the FARQ and other paramilitary groups, both of the Left and the Right.

In 1982 the production of cocaine in Colombia surpassed that of coffee (Colombia is the fourth largest producer of coffee in the world).

In general these warlords were not directly involved in the production and distribution of cocaine and opiates. Rather they protected and encouraged operations in return for a cut in the profits.

Drug cartels supplied (and continue to supply) large quantities of product into the United States, generating fantastic incomes for ruthless drug lords.

For a man like Escobar, dreaming of political power in Columbia, the road to power was paved in cocaine. Whoever controlled the paramilitary organizations controlled the country. Anyone who could dominate the drug trade could dominate them.

Would-be President Escobar therefore had to first reign over the drug lords.

Escobar began his operation in 1975 by buying raw cocaine in Peru and refining it in Medellin. Then it would be smuggled into the United States, where demand for cocaine was high.

Soon Escobar was making $500,000 per trip.

His first air fleet consisted of 9 planes and 6 helicopters.

In 1976 Escobar and a few of his men were arrested on a return trip from Equador, in possession of 39 pounds (18 kilograms) of raw cocaine.

The mugshot taken of him at the time shows a smiling, confident man who appears in total control of his situation.

He attempted to bribe the judges who would decide his case. This failed.

Then his lawyers wrangled for the charges to be dropped. This too failed.

Finally Escobar resolved on a solution that was as simple as it was final. He ordered the murder of the two arresting officers.

Without their testimony the case had to be dropped.

Escobar himself acknowledges this as the point where he realized he could use murder as a tool to what he wanted. He used this tool regularly.

In fact he ruthlessly ordered the murder of hundreds, if not thousands of people in a reign of terror designed to protect and advance his operations.

Anyone who got in his way was removed.

'…I am God,' he said. 'If I say a man dies, he dies the same day.'

More than 3000 died by his command.

He usually killed his victims in one of two ways – *'plata o plomo'*. *Plata* was accepting a bribe. *Plomo* was a bullet.

Escobar's notable victims included Fabio Restrepo, a Medellin trafficker whose demise in 1975 meant that Escobar controlled all crime in Medellin.

Escobar's hitman was one John Jairo Velasquez, also known as Popeye.

Velasquez was born in the province of Antioquia. He joined the army, navy and police force briefly before falling into the Medellin crime scene.

He soon came to Escobar's attention. He chose him as his hitman and brought him into his inner circle.

Velasquez's loyalty to Escobar was total. On one occasion Escobar discovered that Velasquez's girlfriend was an informant.

'You or her,' Escobar told him. 'Do not hesitate a single second.'

Velasquez killed her.

Velasquez was arrested on charges of terrorism, drug trafficking and murder. In 1992 he was imprisoned.

He was released in 2014 He now speaks on a YouTube channel on topics related to crime and politics.

He calls himself '*Arrepentido*' (repentant), though many criticize him for capitalizing on his notoriety.

The demand for cocaine in the United States increased and Escobar stepped up his operation.

He founded his own drug cartel in Medellin, in partnership with a number of other drug lords.

The key members of the Cartel, beside Escobar, were Carlos Lehder, Jose Gonzalo Rodriguez, George Jung and the three Ochoa brothers Jorge, Juan David and Fabio.

Escobar's partnership with Lehder was instrumental in increasing supply to the United States.

Lehder started his criminal career supplying stolen vehicles for his family's used car business. From there he moved into the cocaine trade.

He used Norman's Cay, a small island in the Bahamas, as a shipment base.

The island rapidly became a haven for drug traffickers and a place where they could party.

One visitor to the island described being picked up at the airfield by naked women. 'It was a Sodom and Gomorrah,' he said.

The government of the Bahamas turned a blind eye to Norman's Cay until pressure from the US forced it to confiscate the property in 1987.

The Medellin Cartel organized the shipment of about 80 tons of cocaine to the United States every month.

His methods of smuggling cocaine were ingenious.

One such method involved soaking jeans in liquid cocaine. When they arrived in the United States the dried jeans would be soaked again so that the cocaine could be extracted from the liquid by evaporation.

He was making $420,000,000 a week and supplied about 80% of the US cocaine demand.

Escobar lived in style. He purchased an estate in called Hacienda Napoles in the region of Antioquia, of which Medellin was the capital.

Hacienda Napoles covered 20 square kilometers. There is an old colonial house on the estate, as well as a private zoo full of exotic animals such as elephants, antelope, giraffes, hippopotamuses and ostriches.

The ranch also had a collection of antique cars and bicycles, a kart-racing track, a private airport and a bullring.

In addition there were gigantic statues of dinosaurs constructed for Escobar's son, Juan Pablo.

At the entrance of the hacienda there is simple arch. On top of the arch is a small airplane.

This plane was one of Escobar's first. It was destroyed in a landing accident. The pilot, a friend of Escobar's, died.

Escobar reconstructed the plane and place it at the entrance of the hacienda both as a memorial of his friend and of his beginnings.

Nowadays Hacienda Napoles is operated as a theme park by the Colombian government.

Staff are deterred from speaking about its criminal past.

An Escobar legacy still survives in the hippopotamuses of his zoo. After his death the creatures went feral, living in the nearby waterways and forming a population which may be as large as 30.

In addition, 40 hippos still live on the estate.

The feral hippos terrorize the local population

 And fishermen have called for culls.

In 1976 Escobar married Maria Victoria Henao Vellejo. The two had met in 1974. Escobar was 24. Vellejo was only 13.

Her family disapproved of the relationship but they started dating.

The real nature of their relationship has been a matter of speculation, though Maria stood by Escobar to the end, despite his many mistresses.

Perhaps she loved the life of luxury more than she loved him.

The couple had two children.

The first, Juan Pablo, was born in 1977. Father and son were close, though the peaceful Juan Pablo despised what his father did. He shunned and continues to shun any attempt to glorify his father's career.

After his father's death he went into exile with his mother and sister to Argentina, under the name Juan Sebastian.

He is now reaching out to the families of his father's victims to ask forgiveness on Escobar's behalf.

Escobar' daughter was born in 1984. Her name is Manuela.

Escobar doted on Manuela. He forced one of his mistresses to have an abortion because he had promised Manuela that she would be his last beloved child.

Manuela changed her name to Juana Manuela Marroquin Santos when she accompanied her mother and brother to Argentina. Unsurprisingly, she shuns attention and little is known of her.

Politics

One of the paradoxes of Escobar's life was his popularity with many of the poor in Colombia and especially in his own region of Antioquia.

He was widely regarded as a patron and protector, something of a Robin Hood character.

He brought electricity to isolated communities. He built sporting facilities, provided housing for the poor, and indeed built entire neighborhoods for the poor.

He was often seen walking through the slums, speaking warmly to its inhabitants and handing out cash.

The fact that Escobar made Colombian football is little known outside Colombia.

Before Escobar Colombian football was unremarkable. It wasn't until 1962 that Colombia qualified for the World Cup.

Then Escobar came along. He made Medellin a powerhouse of football.

He provided opportunities for many Colombian young men and a sense of pride for a country mired in corruption and violence.

It was an irony of course, that Escobar was largely the source of that corruption and violence.

His motives were not entirely altruistic, if at all. Football gained him influence and power. He could also launder millions of dollars through football.

Yet the memory of Pablo Escobar divides Colombia to this day. The recipients of his largesse, victims of the grinding poverty Escobar himself endured as a child, look upon him still as their father and champion.

Others see his generosity as a means to build support. While that is undoubtedly true, it is also not impossible to imagine a man who had a passionate hatred of poverty attempting to alleviate it for others.

Many held that Escobar was a deeply religious man. If so, perhaps he believed that somehow his kindness to the poor gave legitimacy to the monstrous crimes he committed.

In 1982 Escobar was 33. He had sworn as a youth that he would be President of Colombia by the age of 30. He was late and needed to make up for lost time.

The only path to the presidency could be through a political party, and the only parties of influence were, as they are now, the Conservatives and the Liberals.

He was elected to the House of Representatives in Colombia.

But there was another reason why he was keen to get into politics.

He was afraid of being extradited to the United States and an elected official enjoyed immunity from extradition by a foreign power.

Escobar knew that the arm of the United States was long. It had its agents in Colombia. It had influence with the Colombian Government and especially Conservative governments.

The United States had another reason for wanting to remove Escobar other than stopping his drug operations.

Escobar was anti-American, echoing the sentiments of many Colombians. If he had any genuine political affiliations they were with the Left. At least, that was the association that best opened doors for him.

The warlords of Colombia were financed by drugs. Whoever controlled the drug supply controlled the warlords, and whoever controlled the warlords controlled Colombia.

Therefore, in order to secure a friendly anti-communist regime in Colombia the United States had to eliminate Escobar.

Elected in 1982, President Belisario Betancur, a Conservative, initiated democratic reforms designed to alleviate the condition of the poor and reintegrate the military movements into Colombian society.

To this end he began negotiations with several guerrilla groups.

He was preparing to deal with the drug lords. He wanted to pass legislation that would allow the extradition of drug lords to the United States.

Escobar and the other drug lords were worried.

In August 1983 Betuncar appointed Rodrigo Lara as Minister of Justice.

Though a Liberal Rodrigo was picked by Betuncar for his tough stance against the cartels. In particular he targeted Escobar and the Medellin Cartel.

He denounced Escobar in the Colombian Congress, citing his involvement in the deadly drug trade. He also denounced him for interfering with politics and the media.

Escobar orchestrated a plot with politicians, drug traffickers and journalists to discredit Lara by creating evidence of his own supposed connection to drug traffickers.

The plot failed. Betuncar refused to accept that Lara was involved in organized crime. The concocted evidence, a check supposedly from a drug trafficker and a telephone call, were soon discredited.

With Betuncar's backing Lara then went after Escobar. He was expelled from Congress and his US visa was canceled.

The cancellation of his visa effectively made it difficult for Escobar to flee the country.

Lara revived charges against Escobar that had long remained dormant, and ordered the seizure of planes and property used for the distribution of cocaine.

Escobar retaliated with typical brutality.

On August 30 1984 Lara was driving down 127th Street in Bogota (now renamed in his honor).

An Escobar gunman, Ivan Dario Guisado, riding in a motorcycle, drew up beside the car and opened fire with a machine gun.

Lara's police escort returned fire, killing Darion and wounding the driver.

The wounded man, Byron Velasquez Arena, later confessed to being offered $20,800 to participate in the assassination.

Lara was taken to a nearby clinic but died shortly after being admitted.

Lara's death shielded Escobar from the government for a time but the Minister of Justice had destroyed his political status.

Moreover, it inflamed Betuncar against Escobar. Escobar's rivals could now also ride on the government's anger in their efforts to destroy him.

Escobar realized this immediately. The day after Lara's murder he telephoncd his wife and sister.

His sister Luz Maria recounted 'When Lara Bonilla was murdered, we received a call from Pablo, and he said we had to leave our apartments in five minutes. So I packed my bags, my children's blankets and we began running, and this lasted for how many years. After Mr. Lara Bonilla's death, we had to run for ten years.'

Pablo himself fled to Panama with his family, where they was protected by General Manuel Noriega, President of Panama and himself a notorious drug lord ironically enjoying the support of the United States.

They escaped in a helicopter flying low so as to avoid radio.

It is perhaps evidence of the danger Escobar felt he was in that he sought the help of a man he did not trust. All the time he stayed in Panama he feared that Noriega might hand him over to the US.

What exactly Noriega had to gain by protecting Escobar is not clear, though we may safely assume that a great deal of money changed hands.

While he was staying with Noriega the President received Alfonso Lopez, a former President of Colombia and Betuncar's Liberal rival for the presidency in the 1982 campaign.

His presence lead to speculation that Escobar was using Lopez as an intermediary to offer to pay the national debt of Colombia in exchange for safe passage back to Colombia.

In fact all cartels were offering Betuncar that deal and they agreed that Escobar should be their spokesman. They wanted favors from the government and in particular freedom from extradition to the United States.

They also wanted amnesty for their crimes and they wanted to be left in possession of their fortunes.

Betuncar sent his attorney general to Panama but he ultimately refused. The price was too high.

Escobar continued to run the Medellin Cartel from Panama.

He and Noriega did not get on. Noriega stole an airplane and $3000 000 from him.

Escobar felt uneasy in Panama and with good reason. Panama was under the unrelenting gaze of the United States.

President Ronald Reagan's Administration was supporting Noriega in his fight against the Sandinistas, the socialist organization that ruled Nicaragua.

The US was financing an alliance against the Sandinistas known as the Contras.

US intelligence presence in the region was therefore intense. If Noriega could demonstrate a link between Escobar's operations and the Sandinista it might become useful for him to hand Escobar over.

In 1984 the US could not identify Escobar in Panama but it was surely just a matter of time.

Noriega fabricated a plot in which Escobar's men attempted to assassinate him and Noriega seized several drug labs.

Escobar fled to Nicaragua but he was flying from the frying pan into the fire.

Escobar was now associated with the Sandinistas and thus liable to be identified and seized by US intelligence.

While loading a shipment of cocaine on a plane Escobar and the drug lord Rodriguez Gacha were identified.

An informant, Barry Seal, had planted a camera on the nose of the plane.

The Reagan administration was delighted not so much by the identification of Escobar but by the establishment of a link between the Sandinistas and the Colombian drug traffickers. These would make it easier to secure funding from Congress for the Contras.

An indictment of Escobar was issued from Miami.

Escobar responded in typical form, assassinating Seal, who was living in Baton Rouge without witness protection.

He also exploded a car bomb in front of the residence of the US Ambassador in Bogota. The ambassador left the country.

Escobar needed to get back to Colombia and quickly.

He founded a pressure group in Colombia, named *Los Extraditabiles*, which opposed the extradition of Colombian citizens to the United States.

In November 1986 he wrote an extraordinary open letter to the Colombian people promising to end the violence in return for freedom from extradition.

In the letter he said 'we prefer a grave in Colombia over a prison cell in the United States.'

So Escobar and his family returned to Colombia. Escobar began waging war against Betuncar's government and its supporters.

He tried his usual tactic of bribery first to attempt to impede legislation that would allow the extradition of the drug lords.

When that failed he resorted to murder.

He murdered a Supreme Court judge. He murdered the editor of *El Espectador*, a major newspaper that supported the government.

The horrific murders continued. In parts of Medellin the slaughter was so great that signs were posted reading 'forbidden to dump bodies here.'

The horror achieved its aims and the extradition treaty with the United States was dropped.

Though the legislature had caved in Betuncar had not. He revived the possibility of an extradition treaty with the United States, referring the matter to the Supreme Court for study.

On November 6 1985 35 guerrillas of the Marxist M-19 movement attacked the Palace of Justice, the home of the Supreme Court of Colombia.

The assailants took 300 hostages, which included 43 judges and the Chief Justice.

Government forces rescued 200 of those hostages, but the siege lasted another day.

On November 7 the guerrillas sent a message inviting dialogue, but the decision had already been made to take back the Court by force.

By the end of the day the Court was back in government hands. More than 100 people died – hostages, government soldiers and guerrillas, including the guerrilla commander, Andres Almarales.

Among the dead were 12 magistrates.

What actually happened during the siege is still not entirely known. Recent investigations suggest that government forces may have killed some of the hostages themselves.

The siege was a tragedy for the dead and their families, a disaster for both the government and M-19, but a triumph for Pablo Escobar and the other drug lords.

All records in the court relating the *Los extraditabiles* – those drug lords under consideration for extradition to the United States- had been destroyed. Pablo Escobar's file in particular disappeared forever.

This destruction of the files was intensely embarrassing to Betuncar's government, which attributed the losses to government gunfire.

However it was widely known that Escobar himself had paid M-19 to assault the Supreme Court building and destroy the files relating to himself.

Escobar's own son confirmed that the attack was paid for by his father.

The siege had profound effects on the Betuncar's agenda. It sank his prospects of achieving peace with the warlords and effectively crippled the judicial system for a time.

Another serious threat to Escobar's interests came from the journalist and politician Luis Carlos Galan.

Galan was a senator and had served as Minister of Education in the ministry of President Misael Borrero from 1970 to 1972.

He had campaigned against Belisario Betancur in 1982 and nominated for the presidency again in 1987.

Galan was determined to put an end to the power of the drug cartels and of the Medellin Cartel in particular.

Galan and Escobar were associates of sorts. Both had been members of the New Liberalism movement, a dissident branch of the Liberal Party. Galan returned to the Liberals after New Liberalism's failure to gain the presidency in 1982.

Galan was charismatic, well-liked and powerful. He was a serious threat to both the Conservatives and the drug cartels.

Indeed he was not only a threat to these but to his own party as well. The Liberal Party had long been corrupted by drug money. If the cartels fell, then so would many of the leaders and powerbrokers in the Party.

Alberto Santofimio was one of those leaders. He had once served as Minister of Justice, which was ironic given what he did.

When it seemed that Galan could achieve the presidency easily Santofimio approached Escobar and asked him to assassinate Galan.

Escobar was probably planning to murder Galan anyway. In any case he was keen to oblige. He was furious with him for the way he had sidelined him in the New Liberal Movement, essentially barring him from a chance at the presidency.

At first Galan received death threats and threats to his children. Then came a first assassination attempt.

Escobar's hitman tried to kill him with a rocket-propelled grenade while he was visiting Medellin on August 4 1989.

The lack of subtlety and finesse in using such a weapon for an assassination was evidence of the fearlessness and audacity of the powers that wanted Galan dead.

After this attempt Galan's aides restricted his travels, but he would not be cowed. He did however accept advice not to go to the town of Soacha on August 18 1989. He was to attend an important football match there and address the crowd, which was expected to be large.

However, in one of those quirks of fate he changed his mind.

As Galan walked onto the platform to give a speech before 10,000 people, a shot rang out and Galan fell and died.

But if Escobar, Santofimio and their confederates believed they had removed the threat to their power they had grossly miscalculated.

The assassination did not cow the Colombian people. Instead it outraged them. Their fury is still evident today.

Hundreds of thousands of Colombians had invested all their hopes in this one man – the alleviation of their poverty, the end of the violence, the end of corruption, the reign of justice. Escobar had stolen something precious from them – hope.

The then President of Colombia, Virgilio Barco told the Colombian people 'Colombia is at war. We are at war with the drug traffickers and terrorists. We shall not rest until this war has been won.'

Barco immediately reinstated the US extradition treaty.

The Liberal Party swiftly nominated Galan's close associate and political ally Cesar Gaviria for the presidency.

Escobar stepped up his reign of terror. Thousands of Colombians were killed in car bombings. The bombs were placed in banks, offices, motels – everywhere.

The aim of the terror was to make the people feel unsafe. They would realize the impotence of the government to protect them and so force it to make peace with the cartels.

Escobar attempted to kill Gaviria as well. Gaviria booked a flight, Avianca 203, which was scheduled to fly from the capital, Bogota, to Cali in southwest Colombia.

The plane was destroyed by a bomb, killing all on board, while it was flying over Soacha on November 27 1989. Passengers and crew numbered 101.

The place over which it was destroyed was surely a reference to the assassination of Galan and a warning to any politician who would dare to take Escobar on.

But Gaviria was not on the plane. He had been warned by security not to board it.

On August 7 1990 Gaviria took the Oath of Office as President of Colombia.

Gaviria vowed not to bend to the power of the cartels. But still the terror continued and the government seemed powerless to stop it.

Gaviria would not bend. Neither would Escobar. It seemed as if the slaughter would continue

But then Escobar offered the government a deal.

La Catedral

Gaviria was not entirely powerless in the fight against the cartels. The savagery of Escobar's attacks was in fact testimony to Gaviria's successes.

Gaviria's attempts to extradite Escobar and other drug lords seemed close to bearing fruit. He was in close cooperation with US agencies.

He began offering immunity from extradition and reduced gaol time to traffickers who gave themselves up.

The strategy met with significant success. In the first few months of 1991 10 traffickers did so.

Three members of the Medellin Cartel surrendered themselves: Fabio and Jorge Luis, and David Ochoa.

This was a terrific coup for the government and a serious threat for Escobar. It now had intimate information about the Cartel and its operations.

The informants would surely be as helpful as they could, for they would be anxious for Escobar to be arrested or killed. Who knew if he could kill them in prison?

Rival cartels also saw Escobar as vulnerable and would undoubtedly take advantage.

In May 1991 an 82-year-old Catholic priest, Rafael Garcia Herreros approached the police with a surprising announcement.

Garcia, a well-known cleric who hosted a popular religious radio show, said that he had knelt down in prayer with Pablo Escobar.

'He is tired of hiding and he believes that Colombia can judge him with wisdom and justice,' he said. He would surrender himself to authorities in return for a guarantee of his safety.

As proof of his good intentions, Escobar released two kidnapped journalists.

The truth was that his enemies on every side were closing in. The Cali Cartel were his rivals, and increasingly more than rivals.

Though Medellin and Cali had cooperated in the past the latter was taking advantage of Escobar's weakness.

Escobar's minions were surrendering to the government or to rival cartels and his daughter had been recently injured in a bomb blast.

The government considered the offer seriously. The press was euphoric, decorating headlines with doves bearing olive branches.

But Escobar had conditions beyond protection for cartel death squads.

He told the government that the prison was to be designed and built to his own specifications. It was to be guarded by men of his own choosing. And of course he was not to be extradited to the United States where he was wanted on eight charges.

Gaviria agreed. The 'prison' was called *La Catedral*. It was less of a prison than a pleasure palace. It featured a football pitch, basketball court, discotheque and bar, as well as the usual luxuries Escobar was accustomed to – jacuzzis, a rotating bed and billiard tables.

Among the extravagances there was a telescope pointed at nearby Medellin, so Escobar could see his daughter while he spoke to her on the telephone.

Escobar received visitors in this prison and there were frequent parties. Prostitutes were brought in and alcohol flowed freely.

The purpose of the prison, as far as Escobar was concerned, was not to keep him in but to keep his enemies out. The government was prepared to accept this arrangement if it meant taking Escobar out of the drug trade.

His prison received its name because of its grandeur and opulence.

This terrible place has now assumed a quiet and peaceful purpose. It is a Benedictine monastery.

The word cathedral is derived from the Latin word *cathedra,* which was a bishop's seat of authority.

La Catedral became Escobar's new seat of power. He continued his operations and for Escobar this was ideal. He still enjoyed the freedom to operate as before and now he enjoyed government protection.

News of Escobar's activities leaked to the press. When Escobar tortured and killed four of his underlings over money in the grounds of his prison the government felt compelled to act.

Two officials went to *La Catedral* as if they were attending the court of a prince. They were the Deputy Minister of Justice and the chief of the prison system.

They both came unarmed and told Escobar that he was to be temporarily transferred from *La Catedral to* a conventional trial for his own security.

Escobar was of course not fooled. He already knew of the plan before the officials arrived. Escobar and his lieutenants debated whether to kill them while his hitman Velasquez waved a submachine gun at the officials.

News of the officials' detention swiftly reached Bogota. Colombian soldiers arrived to capture Escobar and rescue the government officials.

On July 22 1992 the soldiers attacked. Escobar's hostages were rescued, but Escobar himself escaped with most of his men.

Escobar had spent only 13 months of his 5 year 'prison' term. He disappeared into the forested mountains behind *La Catedral*.

It was suspected that a compliant guard force had allowed Escobar to escape. After all, he had chosen the guards himself and possibly had been bribed.

Escobar was free, though hunted by enemies on every side. The government was under intense to capture him. But they needed help.

They turned to the United States.

Search Bloc

The United States Joint Special Operations Command was created in 1980 to plan and execute security operations.

They have been employed in Afghanistan, Iraq, Pakistan, Libya, other areas. The organization has been credited with the killing of Osama Bin Laden in Pakistan in 2011.

The USJSO was assigned to train and advise a Colombian task force called Search Bloc.

Search Bloc had been created in 1989 by Gaviria with the express task of hunting down Pablo Escobar.

Members of Search Bloc were rigorously selected. One of their vital qualities had to be integrity.

They had to be impervious to corruption and fearless in the face of death.

Their commander was Colonel Hugo Martinez.

Martinez made an intense study of Escobar. He knew him intimately, even more than many of his close associates did.

He knew his habits, when he slept, how long he slept, what he would be doing at a given part of the day and what he liked to eat.

He knew Escobar preferred 14 or 15-year-old girls. He knew that he wore white Nikes. He knew the pet name he gave to his wife (Tata).

Martinez was apparently the only police officer who wanted to head Search Bloc. It was, after all, the most dangerous assignment in Colombia. Escobar would undoubtedly have his assassins on the lookout to kill him, constantly.

And Escobar controlled Medellin. A large part of the policed force there was in his pocket and the danger of being handed over to Escobar was great.

No member of the 200 strong team of Search Bloc was a native of the Medellin region. This meant that no-one had local knowledge. Still, there could be no risk of being betrayed by even a single member of the team.

Within 15 days of the search Martinez lost 30 of his men to Escobar's killers.

The casualties became so great that the Colombian police considered aborting the operation.

But the killings only angered the remaining members of Search Bloc and galvanized their resolve. On their behalf Martinez insisted that the hunt continue.

Then during a weekend trip home Martinez was visited by a retired colonel. He told Martinez that Escobar had said he and his family would be killed if he did not pass on an offer of $6000 000 to end the hunt.

Martinez was disgusted and he refused.

Martinez was horrified that Escobar had the means of discovering where he and his family lived, but at the same time he knew that the fate of Colombia was in his own hands.

Martinez immediately informed his superior of the bribe. The two agreed that it was a sign that they were getting closer to Escobar.

Escobar had other worries besides Martinez and Search Bloc.

Individuals whose lives had been savaged by Escobar had begun to band together and their number was growing.

These individuals called themselves Los Pepes, a name which was derived from *Perseguidos por Pablo Escobar*, 'Persecuted by Pablo Escobar.'

Despite the name, not all of all of them were vigilantes. Many were members of rival cartels. It was believed to have funded by the

Cali Cartel, right-wing paramilitary organizations and even by the United States.

Los Pepes was as ruthless as the Medellin cartel. Every day they hunted Escobar supporters and associates and killed them.

They exposed the bloodied corpses for all to see and placed signs on them reading 'For working with the drug terrorist and baby-killer, Pablo Escobar. For Colombia. Los Pepes.'

The terror was effective. Anyone suspected of aiding Escobar was killed. To avoid this fate many surrendered to Los Pepes. Escobar's insidious network disintegrated beneath him.

The Medellin Cartel was effectively smashed, but the ultimate prize, Escobar himself, remained elusive.

The Colombian government decided to invite the United States to help them directly.

There was a secret intelligence unit in Bogota called Centra Spike. It specialized in finding people, and set themselves to finding Escobar.

By now Escobar was continually on the run. His friends and associates were being picked off one by one. There were few people he could trust, and even they could be killed or bought. Escobar no longer had the power, or money, to keep them.

He often slept in the forests of the Medellin mountains. He could not use a telephone or a radio for fear that he would be discovered. Instead he communicated by courier.

On the run Escobar put on 20 kilograms. He could not fit into his regular clothes and had to find others. He whiled away his hours eating, sleeping and hiring teenage prostitutes.

He worried about his children.

Escobar planned to move his family out of the country. However his wife, son and daughter were under the protection of the Colombian government.

Escobar knew that the apartment building where they were living under heavy guard.

He managed to speak a number of times to his son.

Other family members and friends also sought the protection of the government, for Los Pepes were gradually killing off anyone related to Escobar.

Los Pepes also knew where Escobar's family was being held. They could have killed them easily. At one point they fired a grenade from a rocket launcher at the apartment.

But they were toying with Escobar to flush him out. They hoped that he would try and rescue his family. The government too was using the children as bait to bring him out into the open.

The End

Escobar celebrated his birthday on December 1 1993. The following day he was alone in his hideout with his bodyguard Alvero de Jesus Agudelo. His courier Jaime Rua and his aunt Luz Mila, who cooked for him, had gone out after breakfast.

On that day he looked unkempt and disheveled, a shadow of the man who had once terrorized Colombia. His waist had grown, so he bought jeans that were too long in the legs. He wore the leg cuffs turned up.

He wore a blue polo top and wore flip-flops. He was uncharacteristically bearded.

At one o'clock, posing as a journalist, he phoned his wife and briefly spoke to his children.

Martinez had allowed the call to go through so as to be able to trace it. As Escobar talked Martinez was already in pursuit with his men.

Driving up and down the Medellin street Martinez peered intently into the windows of the dwellings.

And then he saw him.

Martinez had never seen Escobar in the flesh, but he instantly recognized him from his photographs, despite the long curly black hair and beard.

Escobar, cell phone in hand, stepped back from the window. He probably recognized

Martinez since he had spent so much time and money fleeing from him.

Martinez knew he had to act fast. Undoubtedly Escobar was even now alerting his gunmen. For every moment he hesitated his own life and the lives of his men were in greater danger.

He radioed all the units of Search Bloc in the area and ordered them to converge on the house.

His men knocked down the door of Escobar's house with a heavy sledgehammer.

Then the shooting started. Marinez's men swiftly seized the first floor, which was empty. They could see that there was a taxi waiting at the rear of the house, presumably for Escobar.

Agudelo, separated from his boss, fled to the rooftop. It was covered in loose yellowish tiles and surrounded by three walls.

By now dozens of Martinez's men were in the street surrounding the house. Some were standing on the tops of cars. They shot Agudelo several times before the fatal shot that caused him to fall to the ground below.

Escobar then appeared on the roof. He kicked off his flip-flops and hugged the walls of the roof so as to avoid ground fire.

There was a Search Bloc gunman on a roof above but he could not get a clear shot.

This break in the fire urged Escobar to make a break for the next rooftop.

Immediately a storm of bullets ensued, tearing up the tiles.

A Search Bloc team had secured the second story of the house and were making tentative steps toward the roof. They thought the gunfire was from Escobar's gunmen and radioed for help.

However it soon became clear that the fire was from the men on the ground.

There was a prostrate body on the floor of the rooftop. The gunfire died down. A shooter from the second floor cried out 'It's Pablo! It's Pablo!'

Men approached the body. A Major Aguilar turned the body over. He recognized the bloody face and radioed Colonel Martinez.

'Viva Colombia!' he shouted for all to hear.

'We have just killed Pablo Escobar!'

Aftermath

Search Bloc's account of how Escobar died has been challenged by rival drug traffickers, intelligence documents and Escobar's family.

On December 5 1993, three days after his death, the New York Times reported that he had been killed returning fire with a 9 mm Magnum pistol.

Some members of *Los Pepes* claim that they were present and that they delivered the fatal shot.

Yet other members of *Los Pepes*, notably one of its founders, Fidel Castano, emphatically deny this.

Escobar's own son, who now calls himself Sebastian, claims that he died by his own hand.

According to Sebastian his father had always told him that if he was cornered he would kill himself.

This seems a bizarre thing for a loving father to tell his son, but then Escobar was an extraordinary person.

In any case it is difficult to imagine how young Pablo could have known that his father actually killed himself.

His body was exhumed at the family's request in 2006 and a bullet hole was found in the right side of the skull, evidence, so the family claimed that Escobar killed himself.

Others have pointed out there was no evidence of gunpowder in the hole, indicating that the bullet that made it could not have been fired at close range.

Even after being shot Escobar would not go quietly. After the chaos and bloodshed he caused one might imagine that his funeral was an austere and private affair, involving perhaps just a priest and a few family members.

Instead there were thousands of mourners, all chanting his name and crowding the coffin.

At one point the mob even grabbed Escobar's silver coffin from the pallbearers and took it themselves to the burial site.

Pablo's widow saw a journalist and screamed 'You killed him!' The crowd looked toward the journalist and made for her.

The journalist escaped but the chaos continued. The people tried to touch the coffin, crying 'You can feel it! Pablo is present!'

A band played a local ballad 'But I keep on being King.'

The chaos became so great that Pablo's own family could not attend the burial.

Escobar was buried in the family graveyard he had purchased in the town of Itagui, just south of Medellin.

It is a quiet and peaceful place and hardly seems a reward for the violent life he led.

Even today fresh flowers are laid on his grave.

Outside Escobar's Medellin Colombia rejoiced.

In Bogota the newspaper headlines proclaimed 'Immortal Joy' and 'Delirium.'

President Cesar Gaviria addressed the people of Colombia, saying that 'Escobar's death was a step toward the end of drug trafficking, and that 'it is possible to defeat evil.'

The killing of Escobar was largely symbolic. The Medellin Cartel was already finished before his death and it was unlikely that he could have revived his fortunes even if he had survived.

But Colombia sorely needed symbols. For decades it had been crippled by war, factionalism, armed thugs and the drug trade. Escobar's death symbolized hope and more than hope. His demise demonstrated the power of the people.

The Cali Cartel, founded by Gilberto and Miguel Rodriguez and Jose Santacruz, who broke from the Medellin Cartel in 1977, continued their operations after destroying their greatest rival.

Escobar has assumed legendary status but few know the names of these men.

Nor do they know that the Cali Cartel became more powerful than Medellin had ever been.

At one point the Cali Cartel was responsible for 90% of the cocaine supply not only in the United States but in the entire world.

The violence of the Cali Cartel was characterized by a horrific form of social values. Elements of society considered '*desechabales*' (discardables) were slaughtered and often left in public as a warning to others.

These 'discardables' included homosexuals, prostitutes, petty criminals, street children and the homeless.

Many bodies of these unfortunates were thrown into the Cauca.

One municipality, Marsella, was bankrupted by the effort to remove corpses from the river and conduct autopsies.

After the death of Escobar the Colombian government and the US could now focus their attention on breaking up the Cali Cartel.

By mid-1995 all the heads of the Cartel had been arrested.

After this the Colombian government successfully broke up other cartels.

Nevertheless drug lords retain influence in Colombia and elsewhere to this day, owing in no small part to the reliance of the many paramilitary political factions which rely on drug money to finance themselves.

In order to fix the drug problem the Colombian government needs to fix the political problems, which are complex.

In 2016 the Colombian government signed a peace accord with FARC and by the end of February 2017 all its members had disarmed.

This is certainly encouraging, though FARC represents just a portion of the many paramilitary organizations in Colombia competing for power.

As of the time of writing Colombia remains the greatest supplier of cocaine in the world.

Cesar Gavirio's term as President of Colombia ended on August 7 1994 when he was succeeded by Ernesto Samper Pizano, whose campaign was financed by the Cali Cartel.

Samper was accused of being soft on the cartels.

Gavirio went on to become the seventh Secretary-General of the Organization of American States.

Hugo Martinez continued with the Colombia police until 2003 when he was elected Governor of the Department of Santander.

He was accused of collaboration with the AUC, or United Self-Defense Forces of Columbia, a paramilitary organization formed in 1997.

He was charged and arrested in 2011.

After most of the witnesses to his involvement with the AUC withdrew their testimony the Prosecution had to rely on the statements of one Colonel Julio Cesar Prieto.

Cesar gave evidence that Martinez had gained political office with the help of the AUC.

Martinez was sentenced to 9 years but served only 4 and half months before being granted probation.

Escobar's son Juan Pablo is now known as Sebastian Marroquin.

After his father's death his mother took his sister and himself to Mozambique. They then visited Argentina and eventually became citizens there.

He has a wife and daughter and works as an architect.

He does not like to talk about his father though he did write a book entitled *Pablo Escobar: My Father*.

The book was published in 2014 . It contains memories of his father. They are told plainly without any attempt to diminish the cruelty and ruthlessness of man.

Marroquin recounts the story of how his father left women's lingerie in his brother Roberto's shower when Roberto's wife came to visit. These horrible pranks almost destroyed their marriage. It was only when the couple was about to break up that Pablo revealed what he had done.

At any time Escobar asked one of his minions, called *El Gordo* to bring him a cup of coffee. Unbeknown to El Gordo Escobar popped Alka-Seltzers in his mouth which caused it to foam when he drank the coffee.

Escobar then accused El Gordo of poisoning him and made him beg for mercy at the point of a machine gun.

According to *Pablo Escobar: My Father* the war between the Medellin and Carli Cartels was started by one of the Cali leaders, Gilberto Rodriguez, refusing to send one of his men to Escobar.

This man had had sex with the former girlfriend of one of Escobar's friends, Jorge Pabon.

Pabon wanted revenge, and Escobar told Rodriguez 'whoever is not with me is against me'.

A few months later the Cali Cartel set off a car bomb in a building where Pablo's children were sleeping.

It is also in this book that Marroquin states that Escobar took his own life.

In 2009 Marroquin made a documentary with Argentinian-born director Nicolas Entel.

Marroquin was very reluctant to make a documentary about his father's life and had refused the approaches of several directors.

However he agreed on the condition that his sister was not shown in the film and that his father's name was not used in the title.

The theme of the film is reconciliation. In the documentary Marroquin visits the son of Luis Carlos Galan to ask forgiveness for his father assassinating Galan.

He also visits the son of Rodrigo Lara, the Colombian Minister of Justice murdered by Escobar.

Marroquin and his mother (then going by the name Victoria Hanaeo Vellejos) were arrested in Argentina on November 17 1999 on suspicion of money-laundering.

No charges were laid however.

The assumption that the Escobar family is still living off criminal proceeds will be hard to shake off.

Marroquin and his family have lived in fear of revenge attacks and kidnapping. At one point a distraught Marroquin even asked the Vatican for its protection.

Escobar today

Pablo Escobar is still very much alive in Colombia today.

In Medellin he is often referred to affectionately as *Pablito*, 'Little Pablo.'

Admirers still place flowers on his grave.

Escobar's face can be seen on t-shirts, coasters, place-mats, badges, posters and walls.

Many can point to their homes which Escobar built and where they live rent-free.

They can show you the schools and the churches he built for the poor, and they tell stories of the people who profited by their largesse.

Whatever they think of his other deeds, they see a man who helped people.

In a country like Colombia where poverty and misery are entrenched in society is irrelevant to his memory that all these things were bought with blood and cocaine.

Even the Catholic Church turned a blind eye to where the largesse that profits their parishioners came from.

One resident of Barrio Pablo Escobar, a neighborhood of Medellin built for the poor by Escobar explained his feelings toward Escobar.

'We respect the pain of his victims,' he said, 'but we ask people to understand our joy and gratitude, what it means to move out from a garbage dump to a decent house.'

Another Medellin resident, selling T-shirts with Escobar's image on them, explained 'People really like them because it's like wearing a [picture] of a Saint you have faith in.'

For others Pablo Escobar was nothing but a murderer and a tyrant who leaves a legacy of evil.

Among them is the son of murdered Minister of Justice Rodrigo Lara.

Commenting on his commercial presence, he says 'In a way it is an example of the triumph of culture embodied by Pablo Escobar, in which profit, making three bucks, is more important than anything else.'

The point is perfectly valid, but, as a state minister's son, he might never have felt the sting of poverty and so not quite understand the attitude of many of the Medellin poor.

Frederica Arellano, son of a man killed on the flight that was supposed to kill presidential candidate Cesar Gavrillia, agrees with Lara, and has an answer to the objection of the poor.

'Personally, coming back home and seeing his [Escobar's] face on the TV screen is an insult, a slap in the face,' he said.

'It is also sending quite a damaging message. It is saying: 'Go and become a criminal, because that way you can make money fast and lift your family out of poverty'.

In 2015 Netflix aired a crime drama series based on the life and deeds of Pablo Escobar.

The show, which continued for a second season in 2016, revived interest in the nefarious drug lord.

Some, including Sebastian Marroquin, have accused the show of romanticizing his father.

Judging from the variety of T-shirts bearing his image (one design has his head on a traditional image of the Sacred Heart of Jesus, hand raised in benediction) and other memorabilia, that accusation might be true.

The truth is that human beings are both horrified and fascinated by the depths to which human nature can sink.

Perhaps for most people, like myself writing this book and you reading it is no more than that.

Yet in countries like Colombia, where poverty and violence have forever gone hand in hand, the temptation to use violence as a tool is perhaps not only strong, but no temptation at all, because violence is seen as a condition of life.

Perhaps this is the most terrifying legacy Pablo Escobar left to Colombia: he bathed the country in so much blood that it knows nothing else.

There are in Colombia brave men and women still striving to show there is a better way.

Voices

In this last chapter we look at some of the sayings of Escobar. Reading them may offer some insight into the man's mind. They may suggest what motivated this evil mastermind.

Afterwards we shall see what others thought of him.

First, from the mouth of the man himself:

Everyone has a price, the important thing is to find out what it is.

Life is full of surprises, some good, some not so good.

Only those who went hungry with me and stood by me when I went through a bad time at some point in life will eat at my table.

Sometimes I feel like God…when I order someone killed – they die the same day.

There are two hundred million idiots, manipulated by a million intelligent men.

There can only be one king.

I prefer to be in the grave in Colombia than in a jail cell in the United States.

All empires are created of blood and fire.

I can replace things, but I could never replace my wife and kids.

I'm a decent man who exports flowers.

I have always considered myself a happy man. I've always been happy, I've always been optimistic, I've always had faith in life because I think the most difficult times always bring something. It brings experience, and it's the greatest thing to have in life.

here are two hundred million idiots, manipulated by a million intelligent men.

I'm sometimes accused of drug trafficking. It's an activity that for the time being, historically, shall we say has been declared illegal. It's illegal at the moment, but in the long run and in the future, we're going to show that it will head toward legalization.

Dirty money is in all economic sectors of the country.

The problem is not a matter of money. The problem is a matter of dignity.

Nothing gives a fearful man more courage than another's fear.

In modern business it is not the crook who is to be feared most, it is the honest man who doesn't know what he is doing.

Now some quotes from others about Pablo Escobar. These are the opinions not of his powerful friends and enemies, but of ordinary Colombians, all old enough to have memories of Escobar.

'Escobar was known as The Robin Hood of the poor. He built and gave away houses for many people. He built parks for kids with scarce resources, football fields, gave away money and sponsored many people who needed help. Those are enough reasons for those who venerate and admire him. Yes, it is true that he did much more than the government did for some cities but that does not justify the bad he did with his way of taking control over the business of drug trafficking. So what happens to a person in their search for control and power that wants to take the whole world on? In reality his good deeds end up being only strategies to camouflage a form of crime. More importantly, the legacy or teachings he left the next generations was bad. They want to live a luxurious life and obtain it the easy way. I refer to those who want to become rich selling drugs, kidnapping, stealing, killing and extorting people. They don't want to study and obtain things through hard work. Those are the reasons that for me Pablo was one of the worst Colombians in our history.'

-Kelly, 30,

'He did a lot of good things. He created houses for the poor and gave houses to many mothers who've never had one. He gave jobs and helped people who needed it. He wanted to change the country and most importantly the government. That's why he got into politics. When he did, he aspired to be a president to change many things to change the country. But, the government went against him and took him out of the running. So he sought vengeance and killed many people. He placed bombs and even exploded a plane. He implemented a lot of violence and many innocent people died. But, I liked him because he was going to take Colombia out of poverty and make it a rich country. The government runs Colombia wrong. Colombia is rich in everything, but the politicians steal the resources. So he got into politics and the Minister of Justice, Rodrigo Lara, complained saying that he had been in jail and was a narco-trafficker. They kicked him out like a dog. That's where he started the war towards its leaders.'

Ruben, 41.

'He is a man who ruined the reputation of a country. Due to him and his people we are known all over the world as a country of drugs and they stereotype us as narco-traffickers. When I lived in Medellin, I lived in fear and terror. I remember each night they would put a new bomb in a different part of the city. He then moved on to other cities like Bogota and Cali. That time marks me because we could not leave the house at night and the number one program to watch in TV was the news. For me the saddest aspect of all was the prostitution and hit men because it is still something common in my country.'

-Natalia, 45.

'He had so much influence in Colombia that he changed a generation. Those people saw how easy drug trafficking was so they didn't go to college or work because it was easier for them to make money selling drugs. When that ended, all those people didn't know how to do anything and they were already in their 30s or 40s. So what happened was that they started becoming hit men or extortionists. Just being delinquents because they didn't know how to do anything. Many people I knew ended up like that. At one point they had money, houses, women, cars and then all of a sudden nothing, begging people for money for a soda.'

Javier, 42.

'Aside from the horrible and terrorizing he did, I liked his personality. He was a person who whatever he thought, made reality. And he had big ideas. He helped do the impossible possible for people. He immortalized himself because of what he did. Despite the years that have passed the people still know who he is and remember the great things he did. Like reconstruct the entire barrio for people of low resources. He had his zoo with some of the most exotic animals in the world and had a huge car collection. Like I said, I like him because what he wanted, he made possible. Nothing was impossible for him'

-Alejandro, 34.

'I think it's impossible to love a man that did so many damage to a country. He's the main man who brought drugs to Colombia. He's the biggest assassin of all. He killed kids, elderly, and teenagers with no signs of remorse. He was dedicated to killing the police, he paid millions to get them killed. He left many children orphans, women and men widows, because he killed with no compassion. For me it's as if he did not exist because he did bad things to our country, our society and his own family.'

-Rubiela, 64.

'At first he was an admirable man who helped many people. He wanted to be Robin Hood. He stole from the rich to give to the poor. When he started wanting power is when he turned into fiend and terrorized the country. It's hard to say if he's a hero or a villain. At first he was a hero and at the end a villain. He put the country at its knee.'

-Daniel, 34.

Al Capone

American Gangster Stories

Roger Harrington

Table of Contents

Humble Beginnings

Although he ultimately became notorious as a crime boss engaged in bootlegging, gambling and various other illegal activities and was named by the Chicago Crime Commission as 'Public Enemy Number 1', Al Capone's beginnings were decidedly humble.

Alphonse Gabriel Capone was born on 17th January 1899 in Brooklyn, New York City. Although many people turn to crime to escape their poor background, this wasn't really the case with Al Capone. His parents were respectable people who emigrated from Italy to Austria-Hungary (now Croatia) in 1893 and then by ship to the U.S.

Father Gabriele was employed as a barber while mother Teresa worked for some time as a seamstress. When they arrived in America, they already had two sons and Teresa was pregnant with a third child. They lived initially in a squalid tenement building near the Navy Yard, a generally rough and noisy area although the family managed to remain normal and law-abiding.

Al Capone was born the fourth of nine children, one of whom died at the age of one. Two brothers, Rafaela James (known as 'Ralph') and Salvatore (or 'Frank'), eventually joined Al in his criminal activities. Ironically, given Capone's later career, one brother — Vincenzo, who changed his name to Richard Hart — became a prohibition agent.

Unhappy Schooldays

Capone attended a strict Catholic school where he struggled with the rules and the brutality he faced there. Despite this, he was a promising pupil at least at first. This all changed, however, when he was expelled at the age of fourteen for hitting a female teacher in the face.

The boy's formal education ended at this point and his descent into a criminal career had begun. The transition was no doubt also helped by the family's move, when he was aged eleven, to Park Slope in Brooklyn. This was a much more ethnically mixed area of New York and it resulted in Capone being affected by wider cultural influences.

Included among those influences was Capone's membership of several local gangs. He initially joined the Junior Forty Thieves and then moved on to the Bowery Boys, the Brooklyn Rippers, James Street Boys Gang and eventually the powerful Five Points Gang in Lower Manhattan. The latter was run by gangster Johnny Torrio, who was to have a huge influence on Capone's life.

Early Career

After being expelled from school, Capone took on various odd jobs in the Brooklyn area, including working in a bowling alley and a candy store. Full-time work followed, primarily at the Harvard Inn on Coney Island, owned by mobster Frankie Yale, where Capone worked as a bartender and bouncer.

Whilst working there, Capone inadvertently insulted a woman patron, resulting in her brother, Frank Gallucio, slashing him across the face with a knife in retribution. This caused three prominent scars on the left side of his face that resulted in the press nicknaming him 'Scarface'. After that, Capone always tried to present the other side of his face to cameras and described his scars as 'war wounds', despite never serving in the military.

On Frankie Yale's insistence, Capone apologised to Gallucio for insulting his sister. Nevertheless, he appeared not to bear a grudge since he later hired Gallucio as his bodyguard.

Becoming a Married Man

On 30th December 1918, aged only nineteen, Capone married Irish Catholic Mae Josephine Coughlin. Since he was under 21 at the time, he required the written permission of his parents before the wedding could go ahead. The couple remained married until his death and had one child, Albert Francis 'Sonny' Capone, who was born just prior to their marriage.

The marriage appeared to change Capone, if only temporarily, and he reportedly worked for a period as a bookkeeper. Within little more than a year, however, he was off to Chicago to work for old associate Johnny Torrio and his career as a criminal really took off.

Moving On

The reasons for Capone's move to Chicago from New York in 1920 are somewhat unclear. There is a belief that the unexpected death of his father prompted a change while there were stories that there was a need to get out after severely injuring a rival gang member. More likely is that he went at the request of Johnny Torrio, for whom he'd worked when aged only fifteen, since he immediately became employed by him on arriving there.

At the time, Torrio operated as an enforcer for crime boss James 'Big Jim' Colosimo. When Colosimo was murdered on 11th May 1920, with the culprits rumored to be either Capone or Frankie Yale, Torrio took over the business.

Capone initially worked as a bouncer in a brothel. Here he contracted syphilis, which went untreated because the symptoms subsided and he wrongly assumed the disease had somehow been cured. It returned with a vengeance later and was to eventually lead to the deterioration in his physical and mental health that ultimately contributed to his early death.

Opportunities Abound

The start of the Prohibition era in 1920 offered great opportunities to make immense amounts of money from illegal bootlegging operations. And Chicago was ideally located to capitalize on these opportunities, being well served by railroads and with easy access to huge areas of the USA and Canada.

Added to that, Chicago was a city that had grown from a mere 30,000 people in 1850 to around three million when Capone arrived. The influx of all types and nationalities provided a ready market for what he was supplying.

Although Colosimo had been active in operating many brothels and gambling dens in the city, he had supposedly wanted nothing to do with bootlegging. Torrio, however, had no such qualms and, on taking over, went into bootlegging in a big way.

Capone's business sense led to him taking over the running of the Four Deuces, a whorehouse, speakeasy and gambling joint that was also Torrio's headquarters. The basement area was reputedly used to torture opponents and those with useful information. Capone soon became Torrio's right-hand man, helping to run the biggest organised crime group in Chicago.

Torrio had a reputation as a 'gentleman gangster' and his style was to avoid conflict with rival gangs, instead preferring to negotiate with them over territory agreements. These attempts failed in the case of Dean O'Banion, the leader of the smaller North Side Gang, whose territory was increasingly threatened by the Genna brothers and apparently with Torrio's blessing.

On Torrio's orders or agreement, O'Banion was murdered on 24th October 1924. O'Banion's close friend Hymie Weiss took over the North Side Gang and made revenge over the killing a priority. That resulted in an unsuccessful attempt on Capone's life in January 1925 and Torrio being shot multiple times twelve days later.

Capone's Ascension to Gang Boss

Although Torrio recovered from his injuries, he retired and handed over full control to Capone. He returned to his native Italy for a period of three years before eventually coming back to the US.

At the age of 26, Al Capone was in charge of an organization, which he referred to as the 'Outfit' that included gambling, prostitution and illegal breweries backed up by a transport network that spread across America and into Canada.

All of that came with protection from law enforcement agencies and politicians, together with a degree of ignorance — some newspapers describing him as a 'boxing promoter' due to him having promoted local fights in order to raise extra money. Capone marked his elevation by increasing the organization's revenue through the use of uncompromising tactics.

Any businesses that refused to deal with him were treated harshly. That generally meant their property being blown up, around one hundred people losing their lives during the 1920s to these bombings.

Capone's hardline approach meant that the power vacuum usually associated with a gang boss's demise never happened. He quickly smashed all the opposition that would otherwise have been fighting for control and established a supremacy that few dared threaten.

In the event, the outcome was a significant increase in brothels and a business that generated revenue of as much as $100 million annually, equivalent to around $1.2 billion today. Capone had in place a network of brothels and speakeasies throughout the city and controlled the sale of alcohol to more than 10,000 speakeasies. By 1929, his personal net worth had risen to over $40 million — a figure that equates to about $550 million at today's values.

Gaining Influence

In order to gain the protection of Chicago city hall for his bootlegging operations, Capone is widely believed to have helped Republican William Hale Thompson gain election as mayor. By 1923, having put up with the corruption of Thompson as well as his alliance with Torrio for eight years, Chicago elected reformer William Dever as his successor. Fearing a crackdown on his operations, Torrio decided a second base was needed and sent Capone to nearby Cicero to establish a presence there.

Building a Political Base

The potential crackdown on racketeering in Chicago brought into focus the importance of increasing protection against the law enforcement agencies. That objective was largely achieved by a combination of bribery and strong-arm tactics.

To protect their gambling dens, brothels and other illegal activities, Capone and Brothers Frank and Ralph attained leading positions in the Cicero city government. This was partly achieved by threatening voters and kidnapping the election workers of their opponents, although Frank was killed in a Chicago police shoot out during this period.

Capone used threats, bribery and violence to move existing gangster gangs aside. This caused a change in political opinion and existing mayor Joseph Klenha, who was up for re-election in April 1924, asked Capone for help. He responded by turning gang members loose on the election.

Klenha's opponent was forced out of his headquarters by gunmen, the challenger for the city clerk's office was pistol whipped and helpers and campaigners were beaten up. Election workers were kidnapped, policemen attacked and voters who were planning to support the opposition were prevented from voting.

The whole election fell into chaos and officials asked for help. As a result, seventy Chicago police officers were deputised and five squads of detectives were sent to Cicero to restore order.

One squad came across three gunmen who included Al and Frank Capone. In the shoot-out that followed, Frank was killed and Al managed to escape unharmed. In common with many such episodes over several years, he was not arrested.

The campaign of violence was effective, however, since Klenha was comfortably re-elected. With Klenha in his pocket, Capone established his headquarters in the Hawthorne Inn and took over the town.

Klenha was again elected in 1928, although this time there was no repeat of the violence due to a large Chicago police presence. By 1932, the electorate had had enough and Klenha was voted out. Capone, however, wasn't overly concerned since by this time he was already serving time for tax evasion.

Back in Chicago, in the 1927 election, Thompson won the backing of Capone, allegedly to the extent of a $250,000 contribution, by campaigning for a wide open city that might even include the re-opening of illegal saloons.

Thompson won by a narrow margin in 1927, helped by a bombing campaign on the 10th April polling day that targeted booths in areas that were thought to support Thompson's rival William Emmett Dever. Also a victim was lawyer Octavius Granadary, who challenged Thompson's candidature for the African-American vote and was shot and killed after being chased through the streets by cars containing armed men.

Capone's bomber, James Belcastro, was charged along with four police officers but all charges were subsequently dropped when witnesses retracted their statements.

Maintaining Authority and Security

For a period, Capone moved his Chicago headquarters to fifty rooms within the luxurious Metropole Hotel. This was a statement of his authority in the knowledge that Mayor Thompson would comply with his wishes. That authority extended to his mobsters carrying official police department issue cards stating that the bearer should be treated with the same courtesy as police officers.

Whilst the actions in connection with the elections served to safeguard Capone's operations, his life was still in danger. Despite this, he was generally unarmed but was always accompanied by a minimum of two bodyguards and even acquired an armor plated car for his protection. He rarely risked travelling during the day, preferring night-time travel as a safer option.

There was also a tendency to get away from Chicago at every opportunity. This often included taking a night train to various cities, booking at the last minute an entire carriage for Capone and his entourage. On arrival at their destination, they'd book into a luxury hotel under assumed names, occupying suites for up to a week.

Creating his Miami Beach Base

In 1928, Capone bought a 14-room house on Palm Island, Florida. It was purchased from beer magnate Clarence Busch for $40,000 and had ten-foot walls behind which Capone could get away from public attention.

It was a place where he could escape Chicago's harsh winters while still being able to direct operations from there, sometimes on the 32-foot cabin cruiser he had acquired. Palm Island was also the place where Capone eventually spent his final days on release from prison.

The purchase of the Florida mansion was partly prompted by a need to break free from the pressures and persecutions of Chicago. It also resulted from a journey between various cities where Capone was greeted at each one by a large police presence and it was made clear he was not welcome there.

Capone liked Florida in general and Miami in particular. This was due to the benign year round weather and the indulgent lifestyle where gambling was everywhere and prohibition was largely ignored.

Planning to establish a base there, he booked into the penthouse suite of the Ponce de Leon Hotel under the name of 'A Costa'. He also rented a house on Miami Beach for his wife and son at a cost of $2,500 per month.

The property was leased under the name of 'Al Brown' as a precaution. Nevertheless, the owners soon found out who the real occupant was and worried about the safety of the building and its contents. Their fears were misplaced because Capone actually upgraded some of the contents to meet his lifestyle needs and ensured all bills related to the property were settled in full.

How the Palm Island Property was Acquired

The Ponce de Leon Hotel was operated by Parker Henderson Junior, who was eager to please and provided favors for Capone, including purchasing a number of guns for him. He also acted as a real estate representative for Capone and helped locate and acquire the Palm Island mansion where he spent his final days.

The mansion was bought on 27th March 1928 but, knowing Capone wouldn't be welcome as a resident, Henderson signed all the papers as though he was the purchaser and owner of the property.

Capone spent $100,000 improving the estate, adding what was at the time the largest privately-owned swimming pool with a filtration system that could handle sea or fresh water. Also added were new garages, a boathouse, decking and gardens. Capone supervised all the work and insisted on the best of everything but, like the house, it was all done in Henderson's name.

To ensure the highest standards of work, Capone treated all his workers well. That included providing them with sumptuous lunches and the result was a renovation project of which he was proud.

It took some time before it was realized who the real owner of the property was. This was despite Henderson transferring the mansion into the name of Mae Capone, Al's wife.

Attempts to Move Capone Out of Florida

Economic events had slowed the property market and a hurricane in 1926 had not helped matters. So it was feared Capone's arrival would make matters worse and turn Miami Beach into a place where people didn't want to come.

Several local groups protested at Capone's presence in Miami, prompting a meeting with the mayor and the Miami Beach city mayor. They appeared satisfied with his explanation that he was there for relaxation and would not cause any trouble.

Although the area was alive with illegal gambling, prostitution and other corrupt activities, to which local officials had turned a blind eye; Capone was accused of bringing in gambling. There was a newspaper-led campaign to get him out and a move by the American League to strip him of his constitutional rights.

The Miami Beach city council tried to sue him while the governor of Florida attempted to have him arrested. This occurred on a few occasions but only resulted in him being jailed once. Constant surveillance failed to curb his activities and endless harassment did not succeed in driving him out. Capone did attempt to improve relationships by hosting a series of goodwill dinners but opinions were too firmly entrenched to change matters much.

Residents campaigned for his removal and various authorities combined with business leaders to support this action. Many of the latter, however, saw Capone's presence as a business opportunity and efforts to move him out failed.

Those attempts included arresting Capone on vagrancy charges in April 1930, a ploy that a Chicago judge repeated in September of the same year. Neither charge succeeded in achieving the desired intent.

Centre of Attention

Although he was undoubtedly a gangster who inflicted pain, suffering and death on many people, Capone didn't really see himself in the same light. He liked to portray himself as a pillar of the community and a benevolent character that helped others, opening soup kitchens during the Depression and making significant donations to numerous charities. That image was, however, the complete opposite of the view of many — particularly the law enforcement agencies.

Well-known for his brutality, Capone was described by the New Yorker in 1928 as 'the greatest gang leader in history'. Against that, he considered himself a gentleman and believed the jobs he provided, criminal though they may be, created an income for people who would otherwise be poor. He liked to be described as some sort of Robin Hood, who gave to the poor at the expense of the rich.

Many people, particularly Italian immigrants, viewed him as a community leader who helped the poor. One of his projects was to provide daily milk to poor Chicago schoolchildren to help prevent rickets. He would send flowers to the funerals of rival gang members and had a reputation for helping people who were in need.

A Sharp Dresser

Capone was a flamboyant character who wore sharp, pin stripe or chalk suits and fedora hats in lighter, contrasting colors, often with a cigar in his mouth, an image on which numerous fictitious gangster characters are based. The suits were in a variety of colors ranging from charcoal through to lighter summer colors, especially when in Florida. The suit lengths were often imported from Italy at a price that was the equivalent of $6,500 each today.

He was generally adorned with gaudy jeweler, which he dispensed with at his trial for tax evasion in order to display a more conservative image. His more human side also extended to a love of fishing, singing and writing music.

Despite his Italian roots and his membership of what was in essence a crime group with a very Italian background, Capone was fiercely American. If at any time he was described as Italian, he would proudly insist that he was born in Brooklyn.

Maintaining a High Profile

He loved his celebrity status and nourished it by always being available to talk to the press. When questioned about his activities, he portrayed himself as a respectable businessman who aimed to satisfy demand and was providing a public service by doing so.

Capone's courting of the press and his quest for publicity were things that later came back to haunt him. In interviews while in prison, he voiced regrets at having spoken so extensively to the press because the high profile that resulted had made him a target and had at the very least accelerated his eventual demise.

As well as associating with the press, Capone attended the opera, ball games and other public events where he generally was greeted with standing ovations and people wishing to shake him by the hand. Numerous attempts to increase his profile included moving the headquarters to the luxurious Metropole Hotel for a time.

For a period of four years, from 1925 to 1929, Capone was the most high profile gangster in the country. He worked hard to cultivate his image as a respectable businessman who cared for the people of Chicago. Throughout that period, however, conflicts between the rival gangs were increasing and the violence was growing, which was at variance with the image Capone strove to promote.

He hated the nickname of 'Scarface' that was given to him by the press, since it didn't fit with the image he wanted to put out. Instead, he preferred close friends' reference to him as 'Snorky', a slang term to describe a sharp dresser, or other criminal associates calling him the 'Big Fellow' or 'Big Al'.

Neither of the latter names referred to his height because, at five foot ten inches, he was little over average height although he was at the very least somewhat corpulent. The reference was more likely to his status as undisputed head of criminal activities in Chicago.

At the height of his fame, around 1927, his notoriety had spread throughout the country and even abroad. Tour buses drove past his headquarters, visitors expected to see him and the police even recruited him to greet a group of Italian aviators on a world tour.

Capone reputedly had a long-held belief that he would have been better selling milk than alcohol since there was a lot less hassle and an enduring demand. He did, in fact, own a dairy farm and sold milk in bottles that were labelled with expiry dates, which is something we accept as a regular occurrence today. Back then, it tied in with his stated wish for all milk sold in Chicago to have expiry dates, resulting from a relative apparently having become ill after drinking old milk and, possibly, simply being part of his wish to be seen as a respectable businessman.

Relationships with his Family

Capone was a devoted family man and tried to keep his home life entirely separate from his criminal activities, an approach advocated by his mentor Johnny Torrio. One theory is that he started or at least escalated his life of crime to provide for his family after his father died when he was only 21. He was devoted to his mother and was in daily contact with her whenever possible.

Although Capone's marriage to Mae endured right through to his death, that doesn't mean he remained faithful to her. His sexual deeds led to his contracting syphilis and he then infected his wife with the disease, never admitting he had contracted it since that would have been an admission of adultery. For the same reason, he never undertook treatment despite suffering flu-like symptoms, rashes and sores as a result of it.

The conflicting views of Al Capone once led to someone describing him as the kind of person who would kiss babies during the day and kill their parents at night while they slept. That probably just about sums up his personality and was reflected in the way he did business, negotiating with a smile on his face but destroying and killing those who refused to do business with him on his terms.

Victims and Events

Throughout Capone's career, a whole string of killings and other unsavory events were linked to his name. He was prone to mood swings and frequent violent outbursts, which with hindsight may have been brought on by the gradually worsening dementia that resulted from his syphilis infection.

According to the Chicago Daily Tribune, 33 people were killed, directly or indirectly, by Capone, while others put the figure as high as 700. The earliest of these killings, on 7th May 1923, was Joe Howard, who attempted to hijack a beer consignment belonging to Johnny Torrio and had attacked Jake 'Greasy Thumb' Guzik, the trusted treasurer and financial expert of the Outfit. There was also suspicion that Capone had been involved in the death of 'Big Jim' Colosimo three years previously.

Removing Rival Gang Leaders
At Torrio's request, Capone was believed to have participated in the killing of North Side Gang leader Dean O'Banion in November 1924. That incident resulted in Torrio being shot in a revenge attack, forcing his retirement and causing Capone's accession to the top job. It also, in October 1926, led to the murder of Earl 'Hymie' Weiss, who succeeded O'Banion as North Street Gang leader and vowed to get Capone.

Weiss was the son of Polish immigrants and had formed the North Side Gang along with Dean O'Banion and George 'Bugs' Moran.

He took over after O'Banion's death and made several attempts on Capone's life in a bid to gain revenge.

There had been a previous attempt on Weiss's life after Capone's driver was tortured and killed. Following that, on 20th September 1926, the North Side Gang made a concerted attempt to murder Capone.

After staging a ploy to draw him to the windows of his Hawthorne Inn headquarters, they then opened fire with machine guns and shotguns. Capone escaped unhurt and, after attempts to call a truce failed, Weiss and a companion were killed and three others injured three weeks later outside the North Side headquarters. The response was to kidnap and kill the owner of the Hawthorne Inn's restaurant, who was a friend of Capone.

Although no-one was ever charged with Weiss's murder, it was widely thought that Capone's top gunman, Jack McGurn, armed with a machine gun, had been one of the two assailants. Trusted associate Frank Nitti was suspected of being responsible for the planning of the hit.

The Killing of Billy McSwiggin

On 27th April 1926, in an event that became known as the Adonis Club Massacre, Thomas Duffy and James Doherty were killed due to their threats against an attempt by Capone and Frankie Yale to bring large quantities of bootleg whiskey into Chicago.

The killings were undertaken by gunmen armed with machine guns. They drove past in five cars and opened fire as members of a rival gang left the Adonis Club bar.

Caught up in the shooting and also killed was assistant state prosecutor Billy McSwiggin, known as the 'hanging prosecutor'. McSwiggin was well-known for going after bootleggers. He had previously attempted to prosecute Capone for the murder of a rival but without success.

Although Capone was suspected but not arrested due to a lack of evidence, there was a big public outcry. That helped to turn public opinion against him and possibly, to some degree, set in motion events that would eventually lead to his downfall.

After McSwiggin's murder, Capone lay low for almost three months. Eventually, he came out of hiding and presented himself to the police. With insufficient evidence to have any hope of gaining a conviction, they had no option but to let him go, thereby increasing even further his aura of invincibility.

Killing for a Purpose

Capone viewed killing rival gang members as an act of self-defense since he was only doing it to protect his business. Although he rarely took part in the killings himself, there were incidences where he was known or suspected of having taken personal responsibility. One of these occurred on 7th May 1928, when he eliminated three men who had been part of a plot to assassinate him.

Former associates, they were invited to a banquet and plied with food and drink. Lulled into a false sense of security, they were tied to their chairs and then Capone systematically beat them to death with a baseball bat in a scene later replicated in 'The Untouchables' film.

Another dozen killings followed over the next eighteen months. Some of these were to get rid of rivals who were threatening the operation. Others were people who had been brought in to kill Capone, who had a $50,000 bounty put on his head by rival mobsters, while some planned to testify against him or did not support him as required.

Capone was rarely personally involved in the killings but ordered others to carry them out on his behalf. An exception came after an assault on friend and accomplice Jack Guzik, Capone shooting the culprit dead in a bar. An absence of witnesses meant he was never charged with the murder but his reputation grew as a result.

As Chicago became more violent, with drive-by killings increasingly frequent and innocent people caught in the cross-fire, Capone somewhat surprisingly acted as a peacemaker. He succeeded in stopping the killings and violence for around two months by arranging an amnesty between the various gangs. However, this was never likely to last long and normal activities soon resumed with street violence and fighting between the gangs.

The Treachery of Frankie Yale
A big problem was the regular hijacking of Capone's whiskey transports. This was largely blamed on Frankie Yale, Capone's long-time associate who was now seen as a rival having turned against him. This was reportedly after the appointment of Tony Lombardo as president of Unione Sicilana, an organisation that supposedly controlled much of the Italian-American vote and from which Capone's outfit received some of its political protection.

Capone had supported Lombardo's candidacy while Yale had backed Joe Aiello. Once Lombardo took over, Yale disapproved of his actions and received reduced income from the Unione. He decided to recover the shortfall from Capone and, being responsible for the safe passage of Capone's whiskey shipments through New York, he instead began to hijack some of them.

Yale was killed by machine gun fire on 1st July 1928 but not before he had ordered Capone's informant against him to be murdered. A gun used in that murder was subsequently found to be one of those acquired by Parker Henderson Junior for Capone and led to Henderson eventually testifying against Capone at his tax evasion trial

The St. Valentine's Day Massacre

The next and most notorious event of all, the St. Valentine's Day Massacre, occurred on 14th February 1929. The North Side Gang, which was now led by George Clarence 'Bugs' Moran in succession to Vincent Drucci, who had taken over on Hymie Weiss's death and then himself been killed, had long been a problem for Capone.

The violence between the North Side Gang and Torrio's South Side Gang (later to become the Chicago Outfit) really grew when the latter started selling alcohol on the North Side's territory. That ultimately led to the murder of O'Banion outside a flower shop that he owned.

The relationship between Capone and Moran gradually deteriorated, with Moran attacking Capone's premises, hijacking his liquor shipments and killing those associated with him. There were numerous attacks and retaliations, including two attempts on Capone's life by drive-by shootings, a form of attack that Moran made popular.

An attempt on the life of Capone's friend and associate, Jack McGurn, at last prompted some action. The plan was to ambush Bugs Moran at a warehouse and garage that served as the North Side Gang's headquarters. Capone's men kept watch from an apartment across the street and, on the morning of 14th February, signalled that they had seen Moran enter the premises.

Some of Capone's men, in police uniforms and a stolen police car staged a raid on the premises and lined seven men up against a wall without a struggle. They were disarmed and then shot in cold blood with machineguns and shotguns.

Six of the men were killed instantly but one, Frank Gusenberg, was still alive despite having taken fourteen bullets. He made it to the hospital but died shortly afterwards.

The main problem for Capone was that Moran, despite the information given to him, was not among the victims. Having seen the police car pull up outside the warehouse, he had made his getaway before the attack took place. All Capone's further attempts to get Moran failed, the gangster eventually dying of lung cancer while serving the second of two ten-year jail sentences for bank robbery.

Aftermath of the St. Valentine's Day Massacre

The atrocity caused public outrage and prompted intense police activity. Up to that point, people had tolerated Prohibition and the lawlessness that came with it. Most of the associated violence revolved around gangsters shooting other gangsters, with usually no direct effect on the general public.

Although this event was really no different, the scale and brutality of the killing caused uproar. Photographs of the aftermath of the attack showed the outcome with gruesome reality, causing a demand for something to be done. That drove President Herbert

Hoover to resolve to make an example of Capone.

Although Capone was suspected of being behind the killings, he was at his mansion in Florida when they took place and supposedly had a note from his doctor confirming that he was confined to his bed. Nevertheless, it is widely believed that Capone planned the Saint Valentine's Day Massacre from his Florida mansion. McGurn was checked into a distant hotel and there was no evidence of either man's involvement, resulting in no-one ever being convicted of the crimes.

McGurn was staying at the hotel with his then girlfriend, Louise Rolfe, who claimed they had spent the whole day together in bed. Nevertheless, the police charged him with the seven murders and subsequently also charged him with crossing state lines with Rolfe, an offence at the time due to her being an unmarried woman. McGurn prevented her testifying against him by divorcing his wife and marrying Rolfe, resulting in all charges being dropped.

McGurn was later named Public Enemy Number Four at the time Capone was Number One on the list. However, he subsequently became ostracized by Capone's outfit and in 1936 was shot and killed.

The main suspects for that killing were Bugs Moran, as revenge for McGurn's part in the St. Valentine's Day Massacre, or the Chicago Outfit because he knew too much about them. McGurn was buried at Mount Carmel Cemetery in Hillside, Illinois, the same resting place as many other gangsters, including Al Capone.

The public reaction to the St. Valentine's Day Massacre added to the determination to convict Capone and was another contributory factor in his eventual downfall. He was summoned to appear before a grand jury in connection with the massacre but failed to attend, claiming he was unwell.

He was finally, in 1931, charged with contempt of court for that failure to appear and ultimately did receive a one-year jail sentence that he served after completing his time for the tax evasion charges. More crucially, since a federal court issued the contempt citation, the FBI became involved and it was their work that eventually brought about his downfall.

An estimated seven further killings took place over the next eighteen months up to 23rd October 1930 before he was found guilty of tax fraud the following year.

The Quest for Justice

Al Capone ruled by terror and murder for many years and was pursued by the police for numerous crimes without success. It is, therefore, somewhat ironic that he was eventually convicted and jailed for something as comparatively simple and harmless as tax evasion.

How Capone Evaded Justice

He avoided prosecution for a long time by a process of bribery and corruption of police and officials combined with intimidating or eliminating potential witnesses. An estimated $30 million was spent in 1927 on bribes to various people who could protect him in some way.

His own employees or associates were either fiercely loyal to him or were too fearful for their own safety to act against him. Although many people knew of his crimes, hardly any of them were prepared to say anything about them. He was also careful not to be linked with criminal acts, ensured alibis were watertight and had no properties registered in his name.

Capone dealt exclusively in cash, having no bank account in his name and apparently only ever signing one cheque (for a gambling debt), so that no transactions could be traced back to him. Nevertheless, the case against him was building slowly (the one cheque in his name being part of the evidence) and the outcome seemed increasingly inevitable.

Gaining the First Convictions

Public outcry against his activities became so great that, in March 1929, President Herbert Hoover insisted to Secretary of the Treasury Andrew Mellon that Capone must be jailed. That started the process that would eventually lead to him being convicted of tax evasion.

Prior to that, Capone's first conviction for a criminal offence came in May 1929 after he was arrested in Philadelphia for carrying a concealed weapon while on his way back from a meeting of crime bosses in Atlantic City, New Jersey. He was convicted and sentenced, within sixteen hours of his arrest, to one year in jail but was freed in March 1930 for good behavior.

One month later, Capone was named Public Enemy Number 1 by the Chicago Crime Commission when it released its first list of wanted criminals. This didn't help the reputation of a man who wanted to be viewed as a solid citizen and businessman.

The Role of Eliot Ness

Federal agent Eliot Ness has been widely credited with bringing about Capone's downfall. That's largely due to his memoirs, 'The Untouchables', which subsequently gave rise to a successful TV series and film, although it is now accepted that his role was somewhat exaggerated. The responsibility for this is largely accredited to co-author Oscar Fraley, who was the source of many of the 'facts' in the book.

Ness's small team of prohibition agents was labelled 'the Untouchables' because they supposedly could not be bribed. They raided illegal breweries and other illicit operations and were involved in Capone's indictment for prohibition violations when he was arrested after testifying to a grand jury on 27th March 1929.

Indeed, Ness's team was able to assemble a bootlegging indictment against Capone that ran to 5,000 charges. That work went to waste to some degree when the decision was later taken to prosecute on tax evasion charges instead.

Ness did succeed in angering Capone greatly by destroying or seizing millions of dollars' worth of brewing equipment, destroying thousands of gallons of alcohol, closing some large breweries and damaging his bootlegging business by exposing prohibition violations. A lot of the increased activity was undertaken after Capone murdered a friend of Ness.

Ness's Innovative Methods

Ness was at the very least innovative in his methods and beliefs. His squad cars were painted in easily recognizable colors and had two-way radios to make communication easy. He pioneered forensic science, with an emphasis on ballistic tests and soil samples, and made use of wiretapping to gather evidence.

His battle against corruption led to the setting up of teams to investigate the bribery of police officers, the forerunner of today's internal affairs divisions. And his views on alcohol and drug addiction were ahead of his time, believing that they were medical problems rather than being treated as criminal acts, as was then the prevalent thought.

Although Ness was certainly above bribery and corruption, he wasn't quite the saintly figure that was portrayed. Some of the alcohol that was impounded was given away to reporters to encourage them to cover the story and Ness himself was partial to a drink. His later years featured periods of heavy drinking after a spell as Cleveland's director of public safety and a failed attempt in 1947 to become Cleveland's mayor, before his death in 1957 at the age of 55.

Ness's death occurred shortly before 'The Untouchables' book was published Although a lot of the content was fictitious nonsense, the book told a great story and was a huge success. As were, of course, the TV series starring Robert Stack as Ness, which ran for four years from 1959, and the film starring Kevin Costner that grossed $76 million.

The Change of Tactics

One of the reasons that Capone evaded justice for so long was that different agencies were responsible for investigating his various activities and the FBI only became involved latterly. Any prohibition offences, for example, were the responsibility of the Bureau of Prohibition while the killings in the St. Valentine's Day Massacre were not classed as federal offences.

In an attempt to run Capone out of Florida, he was arrested on vagrancy charges in April 1930. In February 1931, he was tried for contempt as a result of him failing to attend a grand jury hearing after feigning illness. He was sentenced to six months in jail but was freed while he appealed the conviction.

This was the first time the FBI became involved in the pursuit of Al Capone, being asked by US Attorneys to find out if his excuse of ill-health was genuine. It proved not to be true since, despite Capone being supposedly bed-ridden at the time while suffering from bronchopneumonia, he was spotted at the race track, on holiday and was even being questioned by local prosecutors during that period. That resulted in him being cited for contempt of court and other charges followed on from there.

Preparing for the Tax Evasion Charge

A lot of the credit for Capone's later conviction for tax evasion goes to Elmer Irey, a United States Treasury Department official who was told by Secretary of the Treasury Andrew Mellon that it was the responsibility of his office to put Capone in jail. He led the Internal Revenue Service's investigative unit that built a case against him. That was only possible due to a change of law in 1927 when the Supreme Court decreed that income tax was due on illegal earnings.

This occurred during a trial against bootlegger Manley Sullivan, who was convicted of failing to file a tax return that showed the profits he made from his criminal businesses. An argument that the Fifth Amendment protected criminals from having to report illegal earnings was rejected by Justice Oliver Wendell Holmes Junior.

This cleared the way for the IRS special investigation unit to appoint Frank J Wilson, their most relentless and aggressive investigator, to investigate Capone. He was to focus on his spending as a means of proving his level of income.

Capone's income was obviously substantial since his net worth was estimated at about $30 million in 1929. Despite this, he had never filed an income tax return.

Capone had long maintained to all who would listen that he was a respectable and successful businessman. The main point he had overlooked, however, was that successful businessmen earn a good income and have to pay their taxes on that income. That was a big hole in Capone's record that the government looked to exploit.

Lavish Spending Was the Key

Capone's income was well hidden due to the lack of a bank account and no record of any assets in his name. Consequently, Wilson's team of five investigators concentrated initially on his extravagant lifestyle and uncovered purchases of Lincoln limousines, gold plated dinner services and jewel studded belt buckles. They also found evidence of the booking of luxury hotel suites, the staging of lavish parties and telephone bills amounting to $39,000.

Such levels of spending could only be possible if there was the income to match it but determining that income was little short of impossible. Although the revenue came from hundreds of sources, there was no obvious documentary evidence and no-one willing to testify against Capone. That was due to a sense of loyalty or, more likely in many cases, a fear of their lives or well-being should they dare to talk.

One who did talk was Eddie O'Hare, an operator of dog racing tracks and patent owner of the mechanical lure used in these events. He provided leads for the investigators but eventually paid with his life when he was shot to death just before Capone was released from prison.

Breakthroughs in the Investigation

The investigation ran for two years and the first real breakthrough, in 1930, was the acquisition of three bound ledgers found in a raid on one of Capone's premises. These ledgers appeared to provide evidence of income from a gambling hall although without conclusive proof that they referred to Capone.

Comparison of handwriting in the ledgers identified the author as Leslie Shumway and, having tracked him down to his Florida home; agents threatened him with a subpoena. Aware of the trouble he was in, with Capone certain to exact retribution if he were to divulge information, Shumway took protection and agreed to talk. He submitted an affidavit where he described the gambling business and admitted he took orders from Capone in relation to it.

Another important witness was Frank Reis, who was named on several cashier cheques that were assumed to be intended for Capone. After spending four days in solitary confinement, he admitted to agents that he was employed by Capone and that the cheques covered profits at his Cicero gambling hall. This evidence was later repeated in testimony to a grand jury.

In the trial that followed in 1931, the ledgers were actually inadmissible due to the statute of limitations. However, Capone's lawyers failed to make the necessary objections, although the ledgers themselves did not prove his control of the business.

Around this time, Capone's Brother Ralph was tried and convicted of tax evasion. He was sentenced to three years in prison and this prompted Al Capone to take action so the same didn't happen to him.

Capone's Crucial Mistake that Led to his Conviction

He instructed his lawyers to regularize his tax situation but, in doing so, gave the authorities the information they needed about his income. Capone was present at a meeting, in April 1930, between his tax attorney Lawrence Mattingly and investigator Frank Wilson when the stated intention was to settle his tax dues.

At that meeting, Capone nevertheless refused to admit the level of his income and grew increasingly irritated as it progressed, eventually issuing a thinly veiled threat against Wilson and his wife. Five months later, on 30th September, Capone's lawyers stated in a letter that he was willing to pay tax on income in a specific number of years.

This letter covered the six years that were in dispute. It offered that he would pay tax on Capone's income in that period, ranging from an admitted $26,000 in 1924 through to $100,000 in each of the years 1928 and 1929.

The government now had the documentary evidence it so badly needed of Capone's large amounts of income over several years. It was a grave mistake on Capone's part and resulted in him being charged in 1931 with tax evasion as well as violations of the Volstead Act (Prohibition).

The charges were backed up by other evidence gathered by Elmer Irey's team, agents having infiltrated Capone's organization at great risk to themselves. One informer was killed before he could testify but the two bookkeepers who had been employed by Capone were put under police protection before charges were brought.

The Charges against Capone
The government initially claimed Capone had a 1924 tax liability of more than $32,000, while still investigating the years 1925 to 1929. The grand jury indicted Capone for the 1924 evasion of income tax two days before

the statute of limitations would have prevented this. Further counts covering the years 1925 to 1929 were added two months later.

Ultimately, the grand jury found Capone guilty of 22 counts of tax evasion in the sum of over $200,000. Additionally, he and 68 gang members were charged with 5,000 violations of the Volstead Act but the tax evasion charges were considered to have precedence over these.

These were reckoned to have the far greatest chance of success since many jurors would be likely to drink alcohol and therefore have some sympathy with Capone's activities. However, such approval was unlikely to extend to tax evasion, which was generally a detested offence.

The Plea Bargain that Failed
With doubts over the six-year statute of limitations being upheld by the Supreme Court and fears that witnesses could intimidated, US Attorney George E Q Johnson arranged a plea bargain that could see Capone being jailed for as little as two years and no more than five years.

Judge James Herbert Wilkerson, however, would have none of this and refused to allow the deal, so Capone withdrew his guilty plea. Wilkerson was keen to stress that there would be no bargaining with the Federal Government and that the parties involved in a criminal case could not determine the judgment.

How Jury Intimidation was Avoided

Instead, the trial went ahead and a vital element was Judge Wilkerson changing the jury for a fresh one at the last minute and sequestering them each night to prevent them being bribed or intimidated. The action came after the Judge learned that Capone's organization had managed to obtain a full list of all the prospective jurors and was engaged in giving out bribes and making threats to get them on his side.

That knowledge was provided by informant Eddie O'Hare to Frank Wilson, who was initially doubtful of the claims. O'Hare was able to provide a list of ten names, however, that matched those on the list of jurors that even Judge Wilkerson hadn't yet been given.

Wilson was worried that all the work done to bring Capone to trial would be wasted but his fears were allayed by Wilkerson, who was apparently unconcerned by the development. On 5th October 1931, the first day of the trial, Judge Wilkerson started proceedings by exchanging his panel of jurors for another at a trial that was due to start that day in another court.

Capone, who had smiled at the jurors as he walked into court with his bodyguards, was visibly taken aback by this turn of events. The 23 charges of tax evasion against him were then outlined in front of the twelve jurors — all men, since female jurors were not allowed in Illinois until 1939.

The Evidence Against Capone

As various witnesses were called, the evidence against Capone slowly mounted. Tax collector Charles W Arndt affirmed that Capone had not filed any tax returns for the years 1924 to 1929 while Cicero citizen Chester Bragg testified that Capone had clearly stated that he was the owner of the Hawthorne Smoke Shop, a Cicero gambling hall.

That occurred during a citizens' raid on the place and the Reverend Henry Hoover, who led the raid, recalled that Capone had threatened the participants. Some of the most damning evidence came from Leslie

Shumway, who had been the cashier at the Hawthorne Smoke Shop. He estimated that profits of over $550,000 accrued during the two years he worked there but was reluctant to identify Capone as the owner, although he did confirm he was in charge of the business.

Crucial to the case was Judge Wilkerson allowing the letter from Capone's lawyers to be admitted into evidence. He over-ruled an objection that, in effect, a lawyer could not make a confession on behalf of his client. This followed agent Frank Wilson's description of Lawrence Mattingly delivering the letter and stating that Capone was willing to pay the tax liability arising from the income shown on it.

Lengthy evidence of Capone's spending was presented by US Attorney Johnson and he emphasized the hypocrisy of someone who, while claiming to be a man of the people, spent obscene amounts of money on himself and gave relatively little to others. More crucially, the high levels of spending were evidence of the income that Capone achieved but did not declare to the tax authorities.

Evidence of Capone's lavish spending came from several witnesses. One of these was Parker Henderson Junior, who had acted as Capone's real estate representative. He recalled that he'd shown Capone several properties in Florida, resulting in him buying the mansion on Palm Island. Another witness testified to seeing large amounts of cash at the property.

Similarly, a clerk at the Metropole Hotel in Chicago told how Capone held lavish parties there and booked the most expensive suites. All of this was paid for in cash, in large denomination bills.

Frank Reis, cashier at the Hawthorne Smoke Shop in 1927, reckoned the profits there that year were about $150,000. This money was used to purchase a large number of cashier's cheques, at least one of which bore Al Capone's signature.

Failure of the Defence Case

Once the prosecution had presented its evidence, the defense took only one day to make its case and did not do a very good job. Having failed to object to the ledgers being brought into evidence due to the statute of limitations, it then presented a mistaken defense based on gambling losses.

It depicted Capone as a gambling addict who had lost the money his business had earned. Since gambling losses could only be offset against winnings, however, this didn't excuse him from paying tax on his business income.

The defense case that Capone had lost $327,000 over six years and this matched his taxable income was totally spurious. In summing up, defense attorney Albert Fink denied there was sufficient evidence of Capone's gross income and accused the government of being determined to convict him at all costs. Whilst pleading that the jury should not convict Capone just because he was a bad person, he also tried to depict his good side and said he was not a tax cheat.

In his summing up, prosecutor Jacob Grossman stressed that Capone's lavish spending was obvious evidence of a very large income and that the letter submitted by lawyer Mattingly proved that Capone knew he had committed tax evasion. US Attorney George Jackson claimed the case would establish whether someone could conduct his affairs in such a way that he was above the law.

The Verdict that Ended Capone's Criminal Career

On 17th October 1931, after deliberating for only nine hours, the jury found Al Capone guilty of tax evasion on several counts. Although he was acquitted on most counts and found guilty of only five, these were enough for the judge to hand down a sentence that was far above the normal level for this type of offence.

He was sentenced to eleven years in jail and ordered to pay court costs of $30,000 and $50,000 in fines as well as the $215,000 plus interest he owed in back taxes. This was the harshest sentence ever imposed for tax fraud, one that visibly shocked Capone and his lawyers.

To appeal the conviction, Capone appointed a Washington-based law firm that was expert in tax law. They filed a writ of habeas corpus, stating that the charges were outside the time limit for prosecution due to the Supreme Court having ruled that tax evasion was not classed as fraud. The judge over-ruled the appeal by deducting the time Capone had spent in Miami from the length of time since the offences.

Effect of the Conviction

That was the end of Capone's criminal career. His role within organized crime in Chicago ceased immediately although the organization he had previously headed simply carried on under new leadership. A succession of bosses followed him, chiefly Frank Nitti, Paul Ricca, Tony Accardo and Sam Giancana from amongst his previous followers.

The level of violence decreased, however, and Capone's successors adopted a lower profile than he had done. With the end of

Prohibition in 1933, the extent of the criminal activities naturally diminished. Nevertheless, the levels of gambling, prostitution and various other illegal activities continued pretty much as before.

One perhaps surprising consequence of Capone's conviction was that back tax receipts went up, both from criminals and law-abiding citizens. That year, the value of unpaid tax filings paid doubled to over $1 million compared to the previous year.

Final Days

In May 1932, at the age of 33 and weighing almost 18 stones, Capone arrived at Atlanta US Penitentiary. A medical examination there revealed that the use of cocaine had perforated his septum and he was suffering from withdrawal symptoms as a result of his addiction. He was also diagnosed as having syphilis and gonorrhoea, the results of his time working in brothels, and which would lead to further deterioration in his health.

His mental health was already showing signs of failing and he was seen as a weak personality who could not deal with bullying. He required the protection of cellmate Red Rudinsky, formerly a minor associate of Capone's gang, which drew accusations of special treatment.

This belief of favoritism was borne out by the conditions under which he lived. Despite his delicate mental state, he was able to use his influence to procure special privileges, furnishings and other items that made his life easier.

His cell had a carpet, personal bedding and other expensive furnishings. There was also a radio and Capone and various inmates and guards would converse and listen to favorite programs. Visitors were plentiful, with friends and family members maintaining a residence in a nearby hotel.

The Transfer to Alcatraz

Partly because of this, and also to provide publicity for the newly opened Alcatraz Federal Penitentiary in San Francisco Bay,

Capone was moved there in June 1936. Alcatraz was a maximum security prison intended for violent inmates or those with disciplinary issues. Capone did not fall into those categories so the gaining of publicity for the new facility seemed the most logical reason for moving him there.

Soon after arriving at Alcatraz, Capone was stabbed and slightly wounded by another inmate. The assailant was James 'Tex' Lucas, a 22-year old Texan who was serving thirty years in federal prison for auto theft and bank robbery.

He turned out to be a trouble-maker after transferring to Alcatraz from Leavenworth, since he was later involved in a work strike followed by a violent escape attempt in which a prison officer was killed. Lucas received a life sentence for that and a spell in solitary confinement.

The attack on Capone, on 23rd June 1936, was, he alleged, in response to a threat to kill Lucas. He attacked Capone in the shower room, striking him with one half of a pair of scissors and inflicting superficial cuts to his chest and hands. For the offence, Lucas lost his accumulated time for good behavior, a total of 3,600 days.

During his time in Alcatraz, Capone remained a celebrity. There were constant questions from the press regarding his well-being, activities and anything else about him. Even many years after his death, the cell he occupied is one of the main visitor attractions on 'the Rock'.

Capone's syphilis caused the onset of dementia and eroded his mental capacity. The doctors tried to eradicate the syphilis with malaria injections, hoping the induced fever would clear it.

The treatment almost killed Capone and he spent the last twelve months at Alcatraz in the prison hospital in a confused state. On 6th January 1939, he was released and transferred to the Federal Correctional Institution at Terminal Island near Los Angeles, to serve a twelve-month sentence for the contempt of court conviction.

Capone was paroled on 16th November 1939 and referred to John Hopkins Hospital in Baltimore for treatment of syphilis-related illnesses. Admission was refused because of who he was and instead he was admitted to the Union Memorial Hospital. There he became one of the first civilian patients to be administered penicillin as treatment for his syphilis, although by now the condition was far too advanced for it to have much effect.

After several weeks of in-patient and out-patient treatment, Capone left Baltimore on 20th March 1940, donating two Japanese weeping cherry trees to the hospital as thanks for the care he had received. He returned to his mansion on Palm Island for the remaining years of his life, passing the time playing cards and fishing. Test conducted in 1946 by his physician and a psychiatrist concluded that he had the mental capacity of a twelve-year old child.

Capone spent his final days being cared for by his wife and brothers. Most of his time was spent wearing pajamas and having conversations with enemies and colleagues who had died years before, some of them on his orders.

He was reportedly paid by the Outfit a salary of $600 a week, which was barely enough to support his family, pay his staff and maintain the property. Wife Mae kept him in isolation during his last years, knowing any loose public statements about his old organization could well cost him his life while violent outburst brought on by his condition would lose him his freedom.

Illness and Death
Capone suffered a stroke on 21st January 1947. Although he began to recover, he then contracted pneumonia and, on 22nd January, suffered a cardiac arrest.

He died three days later at the age of 48 with his family around him and his physician asked if an autopsy could be conducted on his brain and body for the purposes of medical research. This was refused by the family and the body went to the Philbrick Funeral Home in Miami Beach where it was placed in a $2,000 massive bronze casket.

The body was available for viewing by permitted guests only although two funeral home employees apparently took surreptitious photographs of Al Capone lying in his open coffin. Huge quantities of flowers arrived and the funeral service was held the following Wednesday at St. Patrick's Roman Catholic Church.

Final Resting Place

Capone was buried at Mount Olivet Cemetery in Chicago close to his father and one brother. Three years afterwards, to counter the constant attention and the vandalism of the gravestone, all the family remains were removed to Mount Carmel Cemetery in Hillside, Illinois. The original monument was left in place in Mount Olivet Cemetery in an unsuccessful attempt to prevent visitors learning of the new location of the remains.

In a strange twist of fate, Capone died only five days after Andrew John Volstead at the age of 86. Volstead was a member of the United States House of Representatives who, while serving as chairman of the House Judiciary Committee, co-authored the National Prohibition Act of 1916 that bears his name. The act enabled the enforcement of Prohibition, with Capone's subsequent criminal career partly based on the evasion of that legislation.

Mae continued to live in the Palm Island mansion for another five years until she was forced to sell it. She died in 1986, aged 89, but not before she had destroyed all her diaries and private papers relating to Al Capone.

The Capone Legacy

Despite Capone's violent career and the brutality of his past, there is an on-going fascination with his life. Many fictitious characters have been modelled on him and the term 'mobster' or 'gangster' invariably conjures up an image of Al Capone.

There have been plenty of books and articles covering his life and some of these have been made into films. The most well-known of these is Eliot Ness's biography 'The Untouchables', which subsequently became a successful TV series and then a major film. As in many cases, however, the facts weren't always faithfully recorded and the roles of individuals are sometimes exaggerated.

In real life, Capone's influence was enough to change the law in order to deal with him. The 1927 Supreme Court ruling that income tax was due on criminal earnings was intended to help the authorities trap criminals and was instrumental in Capone's eventual downfall.

The End of Prohibition

Later on, the end of the Prohibition era in 1933 was brought about because many Americans enjoyed going to a speakeasy and having a drink. Additionally, it was obvious that Prohibition was actually encouraging criminal activity and many gangsters were getting rich through their bootlegging activities.

So maybe Al Capone's greatest legacy is, ironically, that through violence and brutality, he changed the laws of America. In order to stop him and his peers, activities that he'd undertaken illegally were made legal.

Although there are the contrasting images that Capone leaves behind — on the one hand a do-gooder who helped the poor and on the other a mobster who thought nothing of torturing and killing his opponents — many of his relatives have responded to the bad side. Some have changed their names and moved away from Chicago while others have refused to talk about him or have done so only under the cover of anonymity.

Despite his notoriety as a mobster, one of the biggest ironies of all is that Capone spent longer in jail than he did as a leading criminal. His reign as a crime boss ended after six years at the age of 33. He was then to spend the next seven years six months and fifteen days in prison before his eventual release on parole.

Ongoing Fascination with Capone

The fascination with Capone appears to show little sign of slackening, even seventy years after his death. A recent auction in June 2017 saw a diamond studded platinum pocket watch that belonged to him sold for $84,375.

The triangular watch, on a fourteen carat white gold chain, features 23 diamonds in the shape of his initials, surrounded by a further 26 diamonds and another 72 diamonds on the watch face. Also sold at the auction, for $18,750, was a musical composition — 'Humanesque' — written by Capone in pencil while imprisoned in Alcatraz.

In September 2016, a letter from Capone sold for $62,500 at an auction in Massachusetts. Written to his son from his cell in Alcatraz, the letter, according to experts, showed Capone's softer side.

The Chicago History Museum's website still gets 50,000 hits a month on pages about Capone while visitors to Chicago still drive past his old home and visit his grave site, even though the body is no longer there.

However, the city has made little effort to publicize or preserve the sites associated with Capone, not wishing to draw attention to its violent past.

Capone's Palm Island estate sold for $7.4 million in 2014. It is now available for hire to use for private functions or events, so the fascination with Capone still endures.

Made in the USA
Middletown, DE
10 April 2021

37342328R00137